SPIRIT WISDOM II

*The Enlightened Warrior's
Guide to Personal and
Cultural Transformation*

An Alexander Book

by Ramón Stevens

ISBN No. 978-0-9639413-0-5

Cover design by Andy Hughes

Pepperwood Press
www.alexandermaterial.com

Printed in the United States of America

Contents

Books by Ramón Stevens

Whatever Happened to Divine Grace?

Conscious Life: Creating Your Reality

Earthly Cycles: How Past Lives & Soul Patterns Shape Your Life

Spirit Wisdom:
　　Living Consciously in an Age of Turmoil and Transformation

Spirit Wisdom II:
　　The Enlightened Warrior's Guide to
　　Personal and Cultural Transformation

`Preface

Over twenty years have passed since a spirit teacher I named Alexander first rapped on the portal of my consciousness, offering a brief message that was but a hint of the torrent to come. After his first two books were finished, I launched *The Alexander Journal*, a bimonthly newsletter, to disseminate fresh material as quickly as possible. Published over seven years, the *Journal* offered readers Alexander's insights on a wide range of subjects both metaphysical and down-to-earth.

One of my frustrations in publishing the *Journal* was having to trim Alexander's essays to meet space limitations; sometimes as much as half of an essay would be excised. This book, and its predecessor *Spirit Wisdom*, restore the essays to their original, unabridged form. More, Alexander has reviewed, revised, and expanded each essay for this volume.

From the first, Alexander has warned of the challenges of living in a time of turmoil and transformation. Our times seem especially perilous now, with the effects of global warming becoming increasingly manifest throughout the world; the malevolent threat of terrorism; and, as I write, a global economic crisis. I therefore asked Alexander to deliver new essays on global warming, terrorism, and politics. Despite their disparate topics, Alexander has woven the essays into a cohesive whole, offering some of his strongest warnings yet of the roller-coaster jolts and terrors to come as western civilization declines and falls.

An old Chinese curse says, "May you live in interesting times." That we do; yet, as Alexander underscores, the turmoil of our age can resolve into a transformed society rooted in natural and spiritual principles. My hope is that Alexander's insights help you to navigate our "interesting times" with serenity and understanding.

Ramón Stevens

1

Humankind and Virus: Earth's Primal Partners

In the grand scheme of Nature's design, one principle rises supreme: balance. Great flexibility is built into Nature's systems, allowing for great variability, but any deviation from the balance point will meet with an equal counter-measure to restore balance. This ensures the stability and continuity of natural systems, from amoebas to galaxies.

If it seems that humanity has broken free of Nature's balancing restraint, and runs roughshod over the planet without hindrance or consequence, it is only because Nature's cleverness and resilience elude your comprehension. For the earth system is set up with many checks and balances to ensure that humanity, whose rational mind allows it both to transcend its maladapted form and to manipulate the natural world, never overwhelms the Earth's ability to heal and restore itself. Humanity may be able to control everything it can see, smell, and touch, but Nature holds the trump card: the virus.

Since there are no accidents in the Earth's design, and all of Nature is a pulsing, living fabric of interwoven life forms, the relationship between humanity and its viral partners is no fluke, no thoughtless oversight. Rather, the human-viral relationship is fundamental to the Earth's design. Allowing a rational species into a natural system always carries risks; and Nature must have a means of keeping such a species in check. In addition, as a rational species capable of metaphysical insight, humanity is meant to recognize that the various diseases and infirmities it suffers are symbols of deeper processes. Every disease has a "causative" agent precisely configured to symbolize the personal or collective imbalance which triggers the agent to harm. Recognizing the symbolism behind the disease helps to steer humanity back toward its proper relationship with the natural world.

The Virus Examined

It may seem risible that humanity's seemingly unstoppable conquest of the natural world could be checked by so lowly and primitive a construction as a virus—which one would be hard-pressed to consider a genuine life form—but there is a greater wisdom at work. In order to serve as the ultimate check on humanity's rational brilliance, the check agent must be so simple in design and function that it has the following qualities:

• It can survive for long periods in a dormant state. With no need for specific food sources or environmental conditions, a virus can survive anywhere and always, matching man's global mobility. A virus can reside under a rock, in the air, beneath a snowpack, within the intestines of terrestrial and aquatic animals, or frozen in ice for centuries. Its very simplicity makes it the ultimate survivor in the natural world, for it is infinitely adaptable to any environmental conditions. It can "go to sleep" for years, decades, centuries, then suddenly arise afresh.

• Simplicity means mutability. The more complex a life form, the less able it is to adapt to changing circumstances, for complex organ systems cannot radically evolve overnight. This means a more successful adaptation to a specific locale, but heralds trouble when conditions change suddenly. Simpler life forms can adapt to changed circumstances far more readily; and since the check agent must be able to adapt itself to rapidly changing conditions, it must be as simple as possible. A further benefit of rapid mutability is the ability to outpace man's medico-technological arsenal by constantly mutating into novel genetic configurations.

• Indifference to survival. Every bona fide life form rides a current of vital energy and a thrust toward fulfillment of its highest potential. For that potential to be fulfilled, an organism must survive and flourish. No life form deliberately poisons the ground of its being—no life form save man and virus, both of which carry potential to ravage their hosts and commit willful self-extinction. In the case of the virus, there is no thrust toward fulfillment, no driving desire for survival: once its reproductive onslaught is triggered, and its furious expansion ravages its host, the virus is simply extinguished along with the host.

• The human body may not recognize the virus as foreign. A healthy, well-functioning immune system is designed to recognize all foreign threats to the body's integrity, and to immediately trigger full-scale assault on any invading microbial agent. There are several "triggers" which alert the body that an agent is foreign. These triggers are tripped when microbes with a certain level of complexity—as revealed in their size and the vibrational emanations of their nuclei—invade the body. A virus, by contrast, is so tiny and simple in construction, with no detectable vibrational emissions, that it often slips under the threshold of immune-system recognition. Thus, a virus may survive quietly within the body for years, triggering no attack-and-destroy response.

• A virus becomes reproductively active only when so "invited" by its host's body. Long-term carriers of the HIV virus are testament that a virus can survive for years inside the body without triggering the massive viral replication causing illness or death. There are several reasons for this, one benefiting man, the other benefiting virus. Viruses benefit because their ability to remain latent enhances their zone of contagion; whether airborne or passed through bodily fluids, viruses can insinuate themselves into large populations before the first illness triggers awareness of their presence. Man benefits because carrying a virus is not an automatic sentence to illness or death; an individual must "allow" the virus to switch from dormancy to active replication, a process we will explore later.

It might be apparent that there are curious parallels between man and virus: both stand apart from the natural world, man with his maladapted body and rational intelligence, viruses with their rudimentary, acellular form falling below the threshold of life. In a sense, man and virus are symbiotic partners, in but not entirely of the natural world, the microscopic partner keeping its larger, potentially trouble-making partner from destroying the Earth on which both depend.

Triggering Viral Onslaught

As mentioned, viruses can survive for years within a host's body, to no apparent ill effect. What, then, is the trigger that allows a virus to suddenly reproduce without restraint, destroying the body's cells and organs and overwhelming the immune system? And why can't the body stop the assault once it begins?

As part of the originally established relationship between man and virus, a virus requires the body's "permission" before it can awake from dormancy. The body contains firewalls which prevent viruses from replicating beyond a certain baseline dormancy level. There must be holes in these firewalls before a virus can leap into reproductive destruction.

What are these firewalls? They are chemical, cellular, genetic, energetic, hormonal, and psychological "viral birth control devices" preventing large-scale viral reproduction. Briefly, here are a few:

• Chemical. A well-balanced diet supplies a continuously replenished stream of vitamins and minerals. Ideally, all requisite vitamins and minerals will be present in proper quantity and proportion. When the ideal balance is maintained, the body's fluids carry a certain tone, actually an electromagnetic matrix of harmonious vibration. In very simple terms, this creates a "shield" protecting the body from viral activity. If one or more elements is missing from the shield, there is a chink in the body's armor which can invite viral reproduction. The more vitamins and minerals a body lacks, the more chinks in its armor.

• Genetic. A person's genetic heritage may influence susceptibility to viral activity. In its nucleus, every cell carries a packet of DNA. This genetic material, if within the normal range, emits a vibrational barrier protecting both itself and the larger cell of which it is part. If the genetic bands are weak, broken, or severely abnormal, the strength of the emitted field is compromised, and with it the resistance to viral invasion.

• Energetic. Medicine is evolving to the point where the body is just beginning to be understood as a matrix of energy. The multi-layered auric fields rising above the denser physical body are invisible to the eye and, therefore, are considered nonexistent. In fact, the auric fields are the nexus between mind and body, the intersection of spirit and flesh, and play a profound role in the body's health. A tightly cohesive, integrated, harmonious auric field protects against injury from within or without. Where there are chinks in this armor—emotional trauma, festering anger or envy, hurtful memories, karmic wounds, or contact with others carrying negative energy—viral activity may be triggered.

• Hormonal. This is most relevant in persons suffering constant stress, triggering the body's "fight or flight" mechanism, flooding the blood with hormonal alarm, only to have that rush of strength and alertness wasted and dissipated. Persons suffering constant emotional or physical trauma quickly wear out their bodies by regularly washing them in powerful hormonal defenses. This hormonal imbalance and attendant weakening of the body may invite viral activity.

• Psychological. Mental states are reflected in most of the systems mentioned above, especially the chemical, energetic, and hormonal systems. Prolonged periods of depression or anger dampen the auric fields' natural vitality, upset chemical and hormonal balance, and open the body to infirmity.

Having illustrated the negative effects if these many firewalls are breached, let us sum up with a positive affirmation: When a body is supplied with proper nutrition, forms itself from a sturdy genetic foundation, enjoys dynamically harmonious auric fields, engages its hormonal alert systems only in times of genuine threat, and is guided by a balanced, mentally healthy mind, *no viral agent can awake from dormancy to activity and breach these defenses.* This is an absolute statement and we knowingly include HIV within its reach.

Breaching the Firewalls

Having laid out the many factors which influence whether or not a virus can spring to reproductive destruction within its host's body, we must point out the obvious: it is virtually impossible for any member of an advanced, industrialized society to have all such firewalls fully intact and protective. The assault on every level of your being—psychological, emotional, physical—is so all-pervasive that the body constantly struggles simply to maintain a baseline level of health, with precious little energy left over to restore its firewalls to optimum fortification.

In fact, the body is unable to build and maintain such a level of defense because it lacks the raw materials. The western diet—highly processed, stripped of fiber and nutrients, full of empty calories— places a great burden on the body as it struggles to render what little nutrition is available from the materials given it. The body possesses a miraculous capacity to synthesize elements missing from a deficient diet, but this requires energy then unavailable for other purposes. Add to this dietary deficiency the many other assaults on the psyche and body—from electromagnetic interference to emotional stress to pollutants in air, food, and water—and the modern body's wounded integrity is a welcome mat for viral infection.

In deeper metaphysical terms, you create your own reality, and no one is ever assaulted by a virus or any other agent without agreeing on some level to participate in the experience. Because the human-viral relationship is so fundamental to your existence as a species, it follows that viral infections tend to reflect not only an individual's psychological or bodily states, but larger conditions in society as a whole, with each afflicted individual serving as a unique thread of a larger cultural fabric. A viral plague serves as a red flag that social conditions are inimical to personal and collective health.

A deep (often unconscious) awareness of the cultural disharmony that invites viral scourge, and a personal reason for choosing to participate, constitute the permission granted by a host. Something shifts in the body. The cell wall which previously stood impermeable against viral intrusion weakens. The cell allows its reproductive machinery to be commandeered by the virus, cranking out viral replicas by the thousand. Each newborn copy bursts from the cell and seeks its own host cell in which to reproduce. Conducted on a mass scale, the virus soon overwhelms the immune system and wreaks severe internal damage.

It is crucial to recognize that, unlike some agents of disease, viruses do not attack the body in a specific, targeted way. They do not attack specific organs. They simply reproduce madly, bursting their host cells as they search for new hosts, in the process damaging or liquefying cells and organs. The overwhelmed immune system, working frantically to combat massive, systemic injury, is unable to battle any opportunistic disease agent invading the body. This understanding is important for several reasons.

First, it underscores that there is no malevolent design in the human-viral relationship. Viruses are not set up to target and destroy specific organs or systems; they simply wait for the cue to begin reproducing. Second, it gives viruses great flexibility and adaptability as they need not search out specific areas of the body to attack; more, they can survive in a multitude of animal and plant hosts, not requiring unique and specific conditions to flourish. Third, it makes the process of isolating, targeting, and destroying viruses all the more challenging, for they are not concentrated in one small area of the body; they are everywhere. Again, the point is to have an agent so tiny, so simply designed, so flexible, so quick at mutating and reinventing itself, and so adaptable to an abundance of hosts, that it can serve its purpose as a ubiquitous, immediately available check on human overpopulation and destruction of the natural world.

Going Airborne

One of the greatest fears of virologists everywhere is of a lethal virus going airborne—transmitted through casual contact, through the air, through a sneeze or cough. If there is a saving grace to most viral onslaughts, it is the inability of most viruses to long survive outside a host body. Having come this far, you know this is no accident. Since most viral transmission occurs through sexual contact, there is indeed an element of permission involved in the decision to engage in the virus-transmitting act, even if the permission granted is to something else altogether! It ensures that only those individuals who have agreed, on subconscious levels, to participate in the mass event of viral plague will do so. Frequently, as with AIDS, sexual issues are explicitly woven into the larger cultural meaning of an epidemic.

At the root of it, all viruses spring from a common source, what we might call the "viral template." This template, designed as a complement to the human template, carries all probable potentials of expression. This means that each virus carries the potential for every level of engagement with a human population: (1) latent dormancy; (2) selective attack on already weakened individuals, such as the infirm, elderly, and small children; (3) a broader attack requiring transmission through bodily fluids; (4) first-stage airborne, transmitted through sneezes and coughs, but quickly dying in the air; (5) second-stage airborne, meaning longer survival in the air but requiring that a new host be infected quickly; (6) third-stage airborne, meaning free survival in the atmosphere with no time limit on infecting a new host.

The gradations between airborne levels are not sharply demarcated, but represent a gradual evolution of a virus's ability to survive outside a host body. Because viruses are configured to precisely reflect their symbolic role in personal and collective illness, this evolution is mediated not by the individual virus, but by the bodies of its human hosts. Just as the body must grant permission to a virus to begin its destructive onslaught, so is the evolution of a virus mediated by humankind at the level of the collective unconscious. Even as it appears the virus is invading and destroying the body's cells, at the same time the body is shaping the evolutionary progress of the virus, manipulating its protein coat to enhance or inhibit its ability to survive while airborne.

A viral plague always has a meaning, and that meaning is manipulated by humanity even as it appears to be the helpless victim of viral assault. If it serves the plague's meaning to have the virus remain at the level of intimate transmission—this is especially true where sexual issues are involved—the viral coat will be "tuned" to wither when exposed to oxygen. If a broader, more generalized condition is involved, the virus can become slightly airborne. If a full-scale, take-no-prisoners epidemic would best serve the plague's meaning, the virus is altered to allow easy airborne transmission. In every case, it is humanity, not the virus itself, that determines the virus's evolution. Humankind deliberately, though subconsciously, molds its viral partners to reflect the desired level of infection.

Frequently, a plague begins with a virus tuned to the level of "intimate contact" transmission; if the larger culture awakes to and resolves the issues the plague brings to light, the contagion is contained, the virus goes dormant, and a changed society is set on a higher, healthier path. If the relevant issues are not responsibly faced, humanity "ups the ante" on itself by retuning the virus to allow some airborne transmission. If this larger plague still does not resolve the deeper issues involved, a widespread, global pandemic may be triggered as a means of focusing humanity's attention with the crystal clarity that only mass death can bring.

So every virus rides a continuum of expression, from dormancy to free airborne transmission. Where the lessons carried in a plague are quickly learned and assimilated, the virus drops back to latency. Where the lessons are not learned, or are resisted by many, the virus is promoted to airborne status. Humanity pulls these strings; not the virus, not Nature.

We have warned before that HIV need not remain forever at its current level of transmissibility, the intimate contact level. The AIDS epidemic is intimately interwoven with issues of sexuality, responsibility, love, and tolerance. Much of society has been transformed since the plague's first appearance, evolving from unconsciously ingrained homophobia to conscious acceptance of sexual diversity; the gay community and larger culture have recognized that compulsive promiscuity is not the highest expression of sexuality, and this has helped keep a damper on HIV's more damaging, airborne potentials.

Compounding the issue, however, is that your culture now passes through a difficult transitional phase from a separatist worldview to a holistic worldview; the disparity between the two is so great that a sizable segment of society is reduced to increasing fear and hysteria, clinging ferociously to the old order even as they feel its energy draining from under them. The poisonous energy this faction spews into the cultural atmosphere is substantial, and carries political clout. This powerful consciousness—"We refuse to learn the lessons of HIV and would rather silence and murder its carriers"—perverts humanity's recognition of the meaning embedded in the epidemic, and almost demands that it become more easily airborne. For if the lessons cannot be learned when only a few of *them* are affected, they must be learned when *you* are affected—your children, spouse, siblings, friends, you.

At the same time, most of mainstream society has radically revised its thinking toward sexual minorities and personal responsibility, which alters the virus in a different way. Even as its modes of transmission become broader, HIV's relationship with its hosts becomes more fluid and discrete. In the beginning of the plague the virus was a certain death sentence, for the equation "HIV = Death" was necessary to get the larger world's attention. With that attention won, and with the healthy shift in consciousness toward sexual issues, the virus need no longer carry lethal imperative.

Now it takes its cues more from its individual hosts than from humanity's collective unconscious. It is far more mutable and plastic in its expression, meaning it can remain latent forever, or for decades, or for years, or for mere moments. The automatic death sentence is lifted, and new lessons are now to be learned: about proper nutrition, about cherishing and caring for one's body, about personal responsibility, about the effects of building a toxic society, about the mind's effects on the body, about creating one's own reality. Some go so far as to honor the virus as their life's greatest gift, and from these wise and insightful souls may indeed spring a new order where viruses and their lethal potentials sleep forever dormant.

The Global Picture

Previously unknown viruses pop up with disconcerting regularity, confounding health officials with novel viral agents. The image is of a world teeming with viruses of infinite variety, which will assault humankind one by one.

It is true that viruses are everywhere; they must be, since they are partners with humankind and, as man can survive in any climate, viruses must follow suit. Rather than lying latent in infinite variety, however, most previously "undiscovered" viruses are little more than carbon copies of the primal viral template. Only upon contact with human bodies will that template take a specific form exploiting whatever firewall breaches affect the people in that area. Upon first encounter, such viruses go into dormancy by default. When the natural environment is damaged or decimated, when life is a misery of poverty and chronic hunger, when the thrust toward fulfillment and happiness becomes a crude mockery, then conditions are ripe for humanity to invite its viral partners to "check" itself.

It is a system of automatic checks and balances. The natural world is seeded with viral templates which lie dormant for millennia until the first contact with humanity. Any human population has certain weaknesses in its firewalls, and upon first contact a virus configures itself to take advantage of those particular weaknesses. The virus then goes dormant within its human hosts; as long as the natural environment is largely intact and the culture allows reasonable opportunities for health, happiness, and fulfillment, the virus remains latent.

When conditions of stress in the natural world or in society sufficiently weaken the body's firewalls, the virus awakens to activity. Permission is granted by the individuals involved, who participate for their own reasons, and by the larger body of humanity for the lessons to be learned. If the lessons are quickly absorbed, the virus returns to dormancy. If not, it raises the stakes by becoming ever more easily transmissible until, in its extremity, an entire population is decimated by a free airborne virus. The lessons are still learned, in the sense that the collective unconscious of humanity profits from the experience; but, unfortunately, the individuals involved do not survive to reshape society with their new understanding.

Thus, to the extent humanity lives in harmony with the natural world, honoring its sacred wisdom and keeping human numbers reasonable, viruses remain dormant. To the extent a culture is founded on humane, open-minded principles of freedom and fulfillment, viruses remain in check. But when man runs roughshod over the Earth or embraces cultural principles contrary to natural law, two processes occur: (1) the body's firewalls begin to deteriorate; (2) humanity grants permission to viruses to switch from dormancy to activity. In the long run—over years, decades or millennia—humankind will be restored to its proper place in the natural order, and to a healthy cultural ethos, by its ubiquitous and infinitely clever partner, The Virus.[*]

---

[*] We recognize that there are vast areas we have not addressed in this essay. Plant and animal viruses; immunity; AIDS in Africa; the decimation of Native American populations upon contact with disease-carrying Europeans, to name a few. While we could easily write a book on the topic, we must limit ourselves here to an essay. We therefore focused on laying a foundational understanding of what viruses are, where they come from, and why their "plagues" are actually invited and mediated by humankind for its own purposes; for such material is of greatest interest to a wide readership.

2

Playing the Human Instrument: Using Music for Pleasure and Healing

Of all art forms, music is the "truest." If art's purpose is to bypass the rational mind, stimulate your deeper being with pregnant symbols, and bathe you in eternal truths, then music fulfills these artistic ends with higher fidelity than any other art form. Unlike painting or literature or sculpture, it is intangible; it shimmers in the air and is gone. It resists the rational mind's analysis for it has no substantive form to tease apart in search of the mystery of its magic. It engages your entire body: it can move you to tears, make you dance with joy, march off to war, or forge tribal cohesion.

This last is the reason music so moves and compels you: it literally resonates with your body. Other art forms are drunk in through the senses and rationally processed; music engages every cell, every layer of your energy fields, with its irresistible sway. In this essay we will explore the processes through which music engages and vitalizes the human body.

The Human Instrument

You can conceive of music as the process of one instrument engaging another: a musical source broadcasts vibrational patterns which envelop and engage another instrument, the human body. The human body is composed of layers of vibration; each organ and cell "sings" a distinct vibrational song which may be stimulated by musical patterns. Let us look at a few of the principles governing the human body's vibrational makeup.

As a general rule, the body's core vibrates at the slowest frequency, while vibrational frequency rises with distance from the core.

The skeleton's stiff bones carry the body's slowest frequency; the body's mass resonates at a higher, though still tempered, vibration; and the energy fields expanding beyond the skin hum at escalating frequencies. Layered atop this general construction is a gradual deceleration of frequency from the crown of the head to the pelvis— often depicted in esoteric terms as "chakras" of decelerating vibration. Each chakra is understood to vitalize a certain aspect of human life: from sexual urges at the root chakra, through emotional vitality at the heart chakra, to spiritual wisdom at the crown chakra.

Thus, the human body is a veritable symphony of vibration, miraculously harmonious given the complexity of its vibrational construction and the broad range of frequencies which blend to one mellifluous resonance.

The upper and lower reaches of the body's vibrational scale far exceed the human ear's perception of sound; that is, the body's slowest vibrations throb beneath your ear's awareness, while the high-pitched hum of your auric fields escapes the ear as well. This is one reason why music engages you so completely: it can directly stimulate areas of the body which receive little stimulation from the ear-brain processing of sound.

Let us briefly explore this. All senses perceive a certain range of vibration and send signals of stimulation to the brain. The brain, in turn, modifies the signals into neurological impulses which stimulate areas of the body pulsing at the appropriate frequency. For example, your eyes can drink in a lofty spiritual text, a heart-wrenching romantic novel, or pornography. The brain transforms the raw visual data of the spiritual text into frequencies compatible with the crown chakra, the spiritual center, which forces concentration to the rarified realms of spiritual truth. The romantic novel is processed as denser, slower frequencies, resonating at the heart and mind, fully engaging your body in tingling empathy with the characters. Pornography is processed as slower still, funneling directly to the root chakra, triggering a rush of blood and lust.

Similarly, the ear and brain work in harmony to perceive and process sound vibration streaming from your environs; and to stimulate germane areas of the body as a means of "harmonizing" the body with its environment. If your body is a field of vibration, and it is the nature of vibrational fields to entrain and harmonize their vibrations, then your body quite literally "becomes" whatever sounds your environment offers up. A milieu of sharply discordant sounds, such as a loud manufacturing plant, literally shreds the body's innate harmony, inviting disability and early death. A bucolic setting of babbling brook and wind fluttering through trees restores harmony to a frazzled body. A body exposed to overwhelmingly loud sounds, such as airports or rock concerts, ultimately loses its ability to hear sounds within that range, protecting itself against further assault.

If you conceive of your body as a pulsating symphony of vibration, navigating through a cosmos of widely diverse vibrational environments with which it can entrain and, to some extent, "become," you understand why music is the truest art form. It bypasses the cognitive process through which art is beheld by the eyes, stripped of its symbolic wrapping, and interpreted. Music engages you on a purer level, free of intellectual abstraction; it envelops and stimulates you directly, every strand, every cell. You don't "think" about music's meaning; you *become* music's meaning.

Musical Wellsprings

Two significant influences determine the nature of a culture's music. The first is the Earth's own vibrational frequencies emanating from the core and filtering through the crust to meet cosmic radiation, there to blend in a vibrational soup unique to each area. This vibrational atmosphere determines the broad potentials for life in that area, stimulating some potentials while dampening others. It determines the range of intellectual, spiritual, and emotional experience in a given area. Consider that in a vast country like the United States, the premier venues for art and culture lie on the coasts; a coast being the nexus between oceanic and terrestrial life, and therefore rich with dynamic energy. In addition, the West Coast is underlain with earthquake faults, which shape the Earth's rising frequencies into dynamic and volatile patterns; thus, cutting-edge artists and scientists are naturally drawn to that area.

The other influence on a culture's music is its own condition and values. Generally speaking, a stable, harmonious, and open culture will devise one basic musical form which resonates with all members and serves as a vibrational nexus enhancing cultural cohesion. A culture fraught with conflict, repression, violence, and animosity tends to fracture into subtribes, each with its own signature musical expression. Like other art forms, music may be used to subvert the dominant cultural ethos, whether in martial songs stirring radicals to battle or dirty ditties mocking sexual repression.

Music, then, is humanity's self-generated medium for expressing and affirming cultural identity and cohesion. On an individual level, whenever you play recorded music or an instrument, you generate a vibrational cocoon which envelops you and resonates with your body's fields, thus empowering and energizing you, affirming the "rightness" of your being. Your distress at being exposed to music you don't like—street kids subjected to Sinatra, or sophisticates assaulted by sidewalk rap—triggers a "fish out of water" sensation: for you are, indeed, in an environment hostile to your body's harmony. You naturally seek environments, musical and otherwise, which harmonize with and affirm your body's vibrational essence.

Playing the Human Instrument

We turn now to a more technical discussion of how certain musical tones, chords, and patterns affect the body. This material may be of greater interest to musicians than those who simply enjoy music, but everyone should gain some insight from it.

In the western musical system, the range of audible frequencies is broken down into octaves; each octave spans eight tones. The musical scale contains the notes A, B, C, D, E, F, and G. Notes with the same name, though octaves apart, have similar "sounds" despite the difference in pitch. For example, a G note's next highest cousin vibrates at precisely twice the frequency as the lower note. The two notes "sound" similar because of their mathematically related frequencies.

Each note resonates with a distinct aspect of the human body. Certain chords and chord patterns are most appropriate for distinct styles of music, for they most readily entrain with the body's vibrations relating to the music's theme.

The key of C is an "all-purpose" key for it resonates broadly with the body and its enveloping energy fields; it is the only key that remains entirely on the piano's white keys, avoiding the spicy inflections of the black notes. The key of D hones in on the heart—relations with friends, lovers, and family—and particularly resonates with issues of loss, regret, and mourning. With its related B-minor and F-sharp-minor chords it generates a musical atmosphere to reduce the strongest man to tears.

The cousin keys of E, A, and B are highly stimulative, with E resonating strongly at the root chakra (and we know what that means), while the higher frequencies of A and B chords stimulate a "get up and go" vitality, an animated vigor. These frequencies link both with the brain's areas governing physical activity and with the cells and muscles sustaining vigorous movement. Feelings of lethargy can well be combated by soaking in a musical atmosphere of the E chord family.

By the same token, because these chord patterns entrain with the body/mind's physical activity areas, when they are expressed as minor chords, in a slow-moving passage, they can bring the body to a screeching halt, almost to paralysis. One feels compelled to cease all activity and *listen* while the music sedates the body and soothes the mind.

The key of F, like its cousin the key of C, has a fairly broad range, but it especially stimulates the internal organs, particularly the digestive system. As a major chord it offers a nice balance between stimulation and relaxation. In its minor form it offers a soothing, sedative effect particularly helpful after a large meal. Because it broadly resonates with the internal organs, including the heart, it also has a spillover effect on emotional life.

The key of G most closely reflects the energies of the crown chakra, the spiritual center, the energies swirling about and above the head which lead to the spiritual realms beyond. Though a cousin of the key of C, it lacks C's "grounding" to earth and physicality; it soars free of earthly and bodily concerns, stimulating lofty thoughts and visions. This is the best key to use during meditation, visualization, or any kind of spiritually based work.

We have briefly mentioned how shifting a major chord to a minor chord—just bringing one note of a chord down a half-step—dramatically alters its effect. A bright, cheerful major chord becomes a solemn, lugubrious minor chord. Without going into great detail, a major chord's three sympathetic notes latch onto and stimulate the body and its auric fields in a full, comprehensive way; resonating with body, mind and spirit in equal intensity. A minor chord impairs this harmonious unity as certain frequencies "drop out" and the body is suffused with the sense that "something is missing." Life's full richness has been lost; one almost mourns the loss of innocent wholeness. Songwriters reaching for pathos instinctively employ minor chords.

Beyond major and minor chords, each chord structure carries a unique effect on the body. Adding a seventh to a major chord, for instance, adds a fourth note to the pattern and increases the chord's complexity; this cannot help but stimulate the body in a richer, denser way. Musicians recognize that adding a seventh "spices up" a chord, opening a new level of engagement with the music. The seventh is the jalapeño of musical cuisine.

Of course most music is not experienced as discrete chords, but as a flowing pattern of musical vibration. A well-crafted melody, one fully engaging and compelling its listeners, creates a flowing vibrational sea whose waves peak in rhythmic cadence atop a harmonious chord pattern. Most important is that the changing chords stimulate sympathetic areas of the body, flowing smoothly from one area to another, without jarring shifts. A good song pleases the ears while it massages the innards.

Organ systems, the brain, and auric fields are stimulated by distinct keys and chords, and the most pleasing music offers a pattern of stimulation-rest-stimulation-rest, alternately engaging and subtly releasing the area of greatest resonance. Abrupt key changes or dissonant chords crashing together drive the listener to distraction because so many different areas of the bodily and auric fields are suddenly assaulted with stimulation, then abandoned, in a chaotic jumble of noise.

Each young generation's music often feels like musical blitzkrieg to parents and elders, for the driving sexual rhythms and turbulent discordance precisely reflect the energies of youth, not of staid middle age. By the same token, store owners have discovered that playing music of the fifties scatters youthful congregations as from the gates of Hell.

Just as different keys and chord patterns stimulate different areas of the body and energy fields, so does rhythm carry an effect on various elements of the body. As a general rule, the faster the beat, the "lower" or more "grounded" the area stimulated will be; while slower pacing stimulates the cognitive and spiritual aspects of being. This may seem a curious paradox, since vibration accelerates from root chakra to crown, but the explanation lies in the lower body's attraction to strong physical stimulation, be it a musical beat, a warm bath, or sex. The more insistent and driving a stimulation, the more completely the lower body entrains to it, blocking out higher aspects. Again, the music of youth most often rides a rapid, insistent rhythm which stimulates and reinforces youth's thirst for adventure, action, and sexual license.

The musical choice of cultural sophisticates is the classical symphony, born of earth energies and cultural structures centuries old. Riding atop a more languid pacing, and a complex musical structure stimulating mind and spirit, the symphony is a natural choice for those living the life of the mind, and those whose youthful energies have mellowed into middle age. Quite literally, listening to a symphony two centuries old transports the body to the earth energies extant at the time of its creation, enveloping its listeners with a bedrock stability and comfort. A symphony provides a temporary reprieve from the chaotic, discordant, 60-hertz energies of modern life, soothing its listeners with the harmonious patterns of a prior age.

Taking this a step further, for a century or so you have been able to record music, capturing artists' original renditions of their music. Playing recorded music transports you to the time and place of its recording, as if you were there. If a Beethoven symphony subtly carries the rhythms of eighteenth-century Europe, modern recorded music pulls you right into the recording studio, there to experience in high fidelity the recording session itself. Artists are thus captured holistically—their music, their essence, and their age—all of which flows, richly revitalized, on playback. You listen to Beethoven and capture a faint whiff of his Vienna, but listen to the Beatles and you *become* the sixties.

Musical Medicine

We have seen that music holds tremendous power to affect the body and its energy fields, and that particular keys and chords directly stimulate discrete areas of the body and fields. Let us gaze into our crystal ball and offer some hints of how music might be incorporated into the "gentle medicine" of the future.

First, the human body can be vibrationally "mapped." Healthy or diseased, each organ, each muscle, each blood cell, offers a distinct vibrational pattern. We envision a chamber lined with sensors, in which a patient lies while the sensors read the body's vibrational patterns. The sensors' data would provide a complete map of the body's vibrational matrix, with which healers could readily pinpoint any areas of disharmony. Particularly noticeable would be tumors or other growths emitting discordant turbulence.

Indeed, since a tumor is always "invited" to a given site by preexisting discordance, the presence of such a discordant field would offer warning of incipient tumors even before they manifest. Application of musical tones entraining with the affected portion of the body could heal the incipient tumor before it grows. Of course, as with any disability, a true holistic approach would also look at other aspects of the patient's life to determine the deeper source of imbalance manifesting as a tumor.

Musical medicine would be especially helpful in healing wounded areas after injury. The healing process of a deep flesh wound, for instance, could be accelerated by weaving a pattern of sound which first stimulates the skin, then the muscles involved, the blood and veins, and so on. Damage to the internal organs could be ameliorated not only by enveloping the body in those organs' healthy vibrational patterns, but by tones stimulating blood coagulation, thus slowing internal bleeding. A bone fracture would heal more quickly when bathed in a vibrational atmosphere of sturdy bedrock vibration.

Needless to say, the field of musical medicine would require a cadre of skilled healers not only familiar with traditional medicine's insights into the body's anatomy and physiology, but who also possess a finely developed musical sense. Most healing sessions would involve precise diagnosis of the wounded or diseased area (through mapping of body and fields), following by application of a complex musical pattern composed with great care. The patient's age, mental and physical condition, and injuries would all affect the nature of the musical medicine to be applied.

Once a course of treatment was determined, a personalized symphony would be composed. It would open with a gentle passage entraining with and soothing the patient's entire body. Layered atop this basic theme, a more precisely focused variation would entrain with the area of injury and stimulate it with the vibrational patterns of its healthy, vital self. The theme and variation would flow through the pattern of stimulation-rest, first fully engaging the affected area, then gently releasing it. The intent is that the injured area begin to generate the pattern on its own during the periods of release. Finally, to close the session, the healing theme diminishes as a broader "body massage" of mild stimulation entrains all bodily systems, encouraging them to work harmoniously in promoting healing; followed by a quiet, gentle release fading to silence.

One of the challenges in devising such symphonic healing is that many of the tones involved lie above or below the threshold of audible sound. This is not an insurmountable obstacle, since the healing symphony would be composed through computers previously programmed with the appropriate tones. As musical medicine advances, computers will assume a greater role in crafting healing symphonies. The healer-technician would study a printout of the computer-generated healing symphony and make any necessary adjustments before applying it to the patient.

As an aside, in some ancient cultures which achieved healing systems of great sophistication but never knew electricity or computers, musical healing was performed through groups of a dozen or so healers who would seat themselves around a patient and weave a complex tapestry of sound with their voices. It was understood that the human voice entrained with the human body more fully than a musical instrument could. The limitation of this practice was that the tones above and below audible sound were not recognized, and therefore could not be woven into a sound-tapestry.

Healing with Music Today

You need not wait for some distant future to begin deliberately incorporating music into your life as one element of a healthy lifestyle. With the brief principles outlined in this essay, you have many options available now. If you have trouble with concentration or memory and want to boost mental power, then classical music, with its centuries-old patterns stimulating mental stability, would be appropriate. Spirituality can be enhanced with even loftier, less "grounded" music, such as much rhythmless New Age music produced today. Problems in the internal organs or with sexuality might be treated with regular doses of rock and roll, which entrains with and stimulates the body's lower, denser regions.

Remember that certain keys are more effective than others at stimulating discrete areas of the body. Problems with motivation, procrastination, or low energy levels would benefit from music in the keys of E, A, and B. The key of C offers a generalized "body massage." The key of D engages the heart and relationship issues (though watch out for too many minor chords!). The key of G enhances spiritual growth.

Finally, you need not look outside yourself for musical healing. The human body is a miraculously self-healing organism which can use sound, among other modalities, to promote healing. One of the most powerful healing sounds is "ommmmmm" which, like the key of C, envelops the body in a cocoon of resonant vibration. The simple act of singing generates a soothing vibrational massage from within. Even clapping a steady beat strongly entrains the body and urges it toward unison and wholeness. So clap, sing, strum, and play yourself to healing and wholeness!

Perhaps you can now see why, of all art forms, music is universally present in all cultures and ages. It isn't just a symbolic abstraction beheld by the eyes; it is a vibrational atmosphere which envelops the body, entrains with it, and stimulates it toward harmony (or not!). It is both an art form and a powerful healing tool. Everyone is born a musician, for everyone has voice and hands. We encourage you to pay closer attention to the sonic and musical atmospheres in which you immerse yourself, to use music not only for pleasure but for healing and growth.

3

Cosmic Adventure Travel: Touring the Spiritual Hierarchy

In deepest terms all is One, an interwoven gestalt of consciousness and form springing from the Universal Mind. Yet this is not how you experience reality—with your body neatly bounded by your skin, and a singular life history and temperament forming your unique character. The notion of universal oneness remains a metaphysical concept floating in the ether, while all around you the evidence of your senses affirms a world of fantastic diversity.

Scientists group the world's many species in classifications of increasing size and complexity: each individual belongs to a species, a genus, a family, a phylum, and so on. Each individual creature is both a discrete entity and a member of increasingly inclusive categories of broadening scope. Ultimately, of course, all earthly beings can be lumped under the rubric of "terrestrial life," a single overarching category in which all life is, indeed, "one."

As on Earth, so in heaven. Just as there are hierarchies of increasing complexity among earthly creatures, and ever-expanding families of shared attributes, so is the spiritual realm structured into "levels" whose entities grow in size, complexity, and purpose.

We should affirm that the spiritual hierarchy does not occupy some distant "place," like the Sunday School heaven floating above the clouds. All levels of the spiritual hierarchy blend and interpenetrate one another. What holds them apart as distinct bands of activity and purpose is the vibrational frequency of each level.

Now, frequency in the nonphysical realm differs from your experience, since in the physical system frequency is inextricably bound to matter. In the spiritual realm, frequency refers to qualities of consciousness rather than "higher" and "lower" pulsations. You might visualize the spiritual realm as a vast chorus broken into smaller clusters of stylistic variety—here a barbershop quartet, there a Gregorian chant, over yonder a full-costume opera. Characters are free to flow from one venue to another, contributing to and learning from each genre until they are ready to move on. The greater a soul's progress, the more complexity it seeks, and the greater the number of souls participating in each realm of growth.

So the different "levels" of the spiritual hierarchy are not sharply demarcated planes, but are naturally occurring clusters of entities sharing a common stage of development and purpose. All levels intermingle, just as they swarm through the earth system outside your senses' scope. For the sake of using familiar terminology, we will refer to the various stages as "higher" and "lower" throughout this discussion.

With that said, let us begin at the "lowest" level, the astral plane, hovering just beyond the reach of your senses.

The Astral Plane

The astral plane is the "way station" between earthbound life and the spiritual realms. It is a field of tremendous bustling activity, as one might expect to find "behind the scenes" of the Earth's exuberant and diverse living systems. The astral plane is the portal through which consciousness crystallizes into flesh, and to which consciousness returns upon release of material form. Entities seeking incarnation in a given time and place crowd the astral plane, scanning the available pregnant women for the most compatible match. The astral level also hosts the wandering consciousness of sleeping humanity, gathering to plot the events of the next day, week, and year.

As you might expect, the astral plane carries the slowest vibrational frequency within the spiritual hierarchy. It pulsates just above the frequencies of matter, just beyond your senses' reach, enabling pure consciousness to readily tap into the thoughts and activities of earthbound creatures. This negligible gap between earth and astral levels also eases the death transition of souls departing their bodies. Let us look at this process more closely.

The ease of transition is largely determined by the death experience. A long, lingering illness culminates not in a "moment" of death, but in a slow, gradual release of the body, a flickering between earth and astral levels as vitality ebbs from the body. Those dying such "natural" deaths are often able to report visions of previously departed loved ones, of celestial radiance, of ineffable feelings of warmth and love embracing them, as they ebb and flow between earth and astral planes. When the last flicker of vitality ebbs from the body and washes into the astral plane, the transition is complete.

Those experiencing sudden and immediate death, such as a high-speed car accident or from a bullet, often suffer a bewildering transition bereft of the easy ebb-and-flow of a natural death. Here, consciousness is *propelled* from earth to astral plane like a stone from a slingshot, leaving a disoriented soul to flounder in confused bafflement: where am I?

But only briefly. For the astral plane is "staffed" with entities who act as midwives to crossing souls. While we call them astral beings, they do not naturally reside on the astral plane, but a few levels higher. The natural order is for entities of a given level to serve as guides and mentors to beings a few steps below. This is part of every soul's growth process—tutoring lower-level souls in the knowledge mastered along the path of enlightenment.

The astral beings devoted to midwifing souls crossing the death boundary we call "welcomers." Their job is to ease the transition in any way necessary, to facilitate the shift from a sensory-based reality to a consciousness-based reality. Their first act upon greeting a freshly crossed soul is to open a "channel" to higher dimensions and direct a flow of accelerated energy around the rookie soul. This is experienced as a sudden rush of love and warmth of a purity and intensity never experienced on Earth. This convinces the soul to release any residual regret over leaving the earth plane and usually triggers a great eagerness to move on.

In the first moments after crossing, some souls easily relinquish processing information through the body's senses, while others insist on retaining their "sight" and "hearing" and "touch." Since welcomers have a tremendous store of tricks at their disposal, they can play along with a soul clinging to its earthly senses, and "appear" in whatever form is most comforting. A historical religious figure, a beloved relative, even an animal—whatever best eases the soul's transition. By contrast, those souls easily relinquishing dependence on the senses will encounter their welcomer not as a specific being, but as an invisible though strongly felt "presence." In either case, the dominant feature of the welcoming pageant is the rush of warm, loving energy enveloping the just-crossed soul.

Once a soul understands where it is and that its body has died, its first task is to conduct a life review. Every moment of life is stored within the body's energy fields as a memory matrix; at death, this matrix is propelled into the astral plane as the eternal record of a life. Under a welcomer's tutelage, this memory stream is "played back" and reviewed for moments of significance, especially any karmic ramifications. The playback may be conducted more than once, until the soul clearly absorbs the full meaning of its life actions and whether any karmic residue has been either released or incurred.

While all of this post-death activity occurs on the astral plane, life's other great passing—from soul to birth—is mediated here as well. Every living being emits a steady stream of vibratory information into the atmosphere, a ticker-tape torrent of experience and thought and dreams. Souls nearing incarnation cluster at the boundary between astral and earth planes—in vibratory terms, they decelerate from higher dimensions—the better to evaluate the personality-streams flowing from pregnant women. Once a woman has passed the first trimester of pregnancy and her fetus appears viable, astral souls sift potential matches for the best fit.

Once a match is settled, a soul gradually links with its fetal anchor by projecting a strand of decelerated consciousness into the womb, enveloping the fetus with its signature vibration. The soul does not leap into the earth system all at once, but gradually trickles across the boundary between astral and earth planes. Even for a period of up to six months after birth, a soul frequently washes back to the astral plane to review its reincarnational history and the tasks established during prebirth planning.

The astral plane is a way station, the nexus between Earth and the higher realms, where souls thicken into flesh and then dissolve back to spirit. It is not intended that souls remain on the astral plane for very long; they are either coming or going. Because the astral plane "works" largely the way the Earth works, and because newly crossed souls are often dazzled with their newfound powers of telepathic thought transmission, some souls linger at the astral level for years, even decades, reluctant to release this last vestige of earthly experience. No pressure is ever applied to take up the spirit's higher journey; souls are gently encouraged to move on, but not forced to do so.

These lingering, often malcontent souls can, under certain circumstances, intrude in the earth system, so eager are they to return without first completing the necessary life review and planning. Entities speaking through Ouija boards are often of this ilk, earthbound souls offering gibberish or, worse, foul language and doomsday predictions. Even these amusements gradually lose interest for astral-level souls, and like all souls they eventually pass to the next realm of the hierarchy.

The Expanding Soul

One of the most difficult concepts for earthbound beings to swallow is the gradual absorption of individual souls into greater bodies of consciousness. The fear of losing one's unique personality and identity, of being swallowed up and lost to eternity, often surpasses the fear of death itself. Recognize this fear as the instinctive reaction of the ego to any threat to its integrity. Then recognize that the ego evaporates at death; so there will be nothing to fear, because there will be no*body* to fear for. As a consolation, your "biography" imprinted on the astral plane at death remains there forever as the eternally vital history of your life. However, this is not *you*, in the sense of containing your consciousness, but is simply an energetic record of your life.

The essential you, your core of consciousness, does move on through the spiritual hierarchy and does *actively seek* to contribute to ever-expanding bodies of consciousness. If you look back on your life and recall being three, ten, fifteen, thirty, you agree that these were all "past" versions of yourself; they have been incorporated into who you are today but do not retain their own individual vitality. So it is with the soul: it seeks eternal growth and expansion through blending with other soul fragments into large bodies of consciousness.

At each higher level of the spiritual hierarchy, the number of such fragments within an entity grows. This serves two purposes: the wealth of biographical experience which can be drawn upon expands; and the power and insight of the blended field of consciousness is magnified exponentially. If you know the power of "putting your heads together" with others in sparking enhanced creativity, imagine the force of a thousand souls joined in fevered telepathic discourse!

The Omega Level

The omega level lies above the astral, and is the next stop on the soul's ascending journey. Entities at this level contain, on average, between 20 and 100 soul fragments. These are the intellectuals and philosophers of the hierarchy: they immerse themselves in understanding the principles and forces governing operation of physical systems. The omega level is the hierarchy's university, for souls must completely grasp the immensely complex, interwoven systems which underlie physical reality. Their studies are not broken down into discrete subjects like biology, chemistry, geology, etc., because the physical system is understood as one indivisible gestalt of energy. Instead, the crystallization of energy patterns into air, liquid, and bedrock is studied, especially the ideal balance of elements necessary to sustain animate life.

We should mention that these "omega entities" are composed of soul fragments who have entirely released the earth system. Having grown through the reincarnational cycle from the selfish grasping of baby souls to the quiet wisdom of old souls, and having released all karmic bonds, they now work to release the earth system entirely and move on to other dimensions. Before they can do so, they must master the principles through which physical reality is created.

When a single soul, late of the astral plane, arrives at the omega level with karmic baggage or a less-than-saintly life history, there is no possibility of its blending into a larger entity; it remains enmeshed within the reincarnational cycle. Therefore, an omega entity will offer a tutorial—a much-abridged version of the knowledge omega entities seek to master—so the soul comes to understand how the physical system operates, how karma works, how life tasks are impressed into each lifetime, and what options it has in fashioning its subsequent incarnations. This is a beginner's course in physical reality and human life; a primer to ensure that every soul carries a firm understanding of the greater context in which its past and future lives are embedded.

The mentor-pupil relationship holds on every level of the hierarchy. That is, souls ascending the levels of the hierarchy are immediately engaged by entities holding mastery of each level's special focus, and will be offered an encapsulated summary of the learning to be gained there. If a soul is just "passing through" on its way to another revolution through the reincarnational cycle, this summary will be succinct and couched in simple terms. If a soul arrives as a fragment released from the earthly cycle and seeks to master a given level's wisdom as part of its growth, such a fragment will be "absorbed" into a larger entity, contributing its store of knowledge to the whole and gaining its collective wisdom.

With each step "up" in the hierarchy, involvement and interest in the earth system wane. Earth is but one small venue available to consciousness seeking physical experience; even the totality of all physical systems is one small corner of activity. Once a soul has completed its reincarnational cycle, and contributes its store of experience to ever-expanding bodies of consciousness, the attachment to Earth, and the learning to be gleaned from earth experience, lessen. As we have seen, the astral level is intimately connected with the everyday bustle of the earth system, managing its flow of souls in and out of flesh. At the omega level, a more abstract, cerebral approach governs, where the underlying mechanics of sustaining the physical system are of greater interest.

The Theta Level

Above the omega lies the theta level, another great step away from earth mechanics and toward greater abstraction. Here, after mastery of the omega level's knowledge, the scope broadens to a spacious appraisal of the creation, operation, and cessation of entire systems of activity, the physical system being but one such domain.

Consider, as an example, the relationship between consciousness and matter as you experience it—though you take the parameters of your system for granted and perhaps have never given it any thought. Within a certain range, consciousness affects matter. The most obvious example is your body's receptivity to chronic negative thought patterns, which may manifest as disease; conversely, a flood of positive, healing thoughts can restore the body's health. Some claim the power of bending spoons or stopping clocks with their mental powers; this steps over the boundary of the commonly accepted limits to the influence of mind on matter. So there is a built-in relationship between consciousness and matter where the mind is granted some power to affect matter, but only within a limited range.

This relationship between mind and matter is but one of the parameters "set up" within each physical system. In other systems, consciousness is so powerful and matter so receptive to its sway that the beings there need no flesh-and-blood bodies; they manipulate their environment through focused intention alone. At the other end of the spectrum are systems where consciousness is so sluggish and matter so impervious to its influence that it is only with difficulty that one could convince one's hand to pick up a spoon, much less expect it to bend through sheer force of will.

This spectrum—from stark duality of mind and matter to their intimate synergy—is but one of the myriad parameters involved in establishing physical systems. Theta entities study the historical experiences of systems in all their parameters, to judge which seem to offer the greatest opportunities for growth—for growth, after all, is the ultimate purpose of existence. A system in which life is too easy offers only superficial experience, while a system fraught with immense challenge crushes too many souls in despair. By tweaking and adjusting the various parameters governing physical systems, theta entities can study diverse "workshops" of experience.

Physical systems do not exist for their own benefit, of course, but as venues of activity for bodies of consciousness seeking matter-based experience. Thus, theta entities are intimately involved in the relationship between consciousness and matter, and focus especially on those venues where conditions support a profusion of animate life. This requires a mastery of the omega-level "mechanics" as background, upon which theta entities build their study of animate life and its many permutations. Because humanity is a special case, radically standing apart from other species with its rational/mythic/emotional life, some theta entities specialize in human life, including its emphasis on relationships and the operation of the reincarnational cycle.

Reincarnation is far too vast a subject to delve into here, but we might briefly mention that it is a far messier and more convoluted process than the common notion of souls leaping from carcass to fetus and magically working out their past difficulties. Because free will is the cornerstone of your system, each incarnation is free to do whatever it pleases—including adding to its karmic burdens rather than releasing them, or failing to resolve karmic debts which its higher self intended it to. The theta entities come into the picture as the guides leading souls through the process of recasting their karmic ties into fresh lifetimes.

As a soul ascends through the astral and omega levels, it understands the meaning of its just-released lifetime and how physical reality works. At the theta level, any souls bound to each other through earthbound negativity will meet after their deaths to review their karmic bond and, with a theta entity's counsel, to recast that bond into a new alliance offering potential resolution.

Souls within the reincarnational cycle lack the wisdom and knowledge to hammer these complex and intricate relationships together on their own, and theta entities help by offering their wisdom to less-evolved souls. Each reincarnational relationship is an immensely complex blending of private and mutual purpose, with no guarantee that the anticipated resolution will result. With their vast store of human experience—theta entities usually contain between 500 and 1,000 soul fragments—theta entities juggle the myriad factors involved and fashion a relationship offering at least a possibility of karmic resolution.

The theta level is the highest to have any direct involvement with earthly affairs, with the churning tumult of life and love in which you are immersed. Theta guides' sagacious counsel offered to karmically bound souls is the apex of the reincarnational cycle— from that point, soul fragments head "downward" to the astral plane to approach reincarnation. Above the theta level, Earth and all material systems become even more abstract and remote, as other dimensions offer expanding opportunities for growth and wisdom.

The Zeta Level

Beyond the theta level lie infinite gradations of mind, ever-expanding aggregations of consciousness ultimately leading back to the undifferentiated Universal Mind. These realms, if they hold knowledge of Earth at all, do so only as a distant awareness held by their soul fragments, a few highlights of lives spent in human or animal form, diluted by the vast experience gained in other realms. There is one exception to this vast gulf between earth and higher realms, which we term the zeta level. This is the level from which we—and many other entities—communicate.

Having passed through and mastered the knowledge of the astral, omega, theta, and other levels, zeta-level entities are a unique lot in that they participate in one final "altruistic" venture with Earth before releasing all involvement. To do so requires, first, that entities at this level have experienced life in human form, so they retain knowledge of how the system operates from the perspective of those enmeshed within it; and, almost always, that they shared a prior life-time with their present human hosts, creating a "bridge" of inter-twined consciousness and experience which serves as the nexus of the relationship.

The zeta level offers its entities an opportunity to zero in on and closely observe the workings of one planet within the physical system, as a "case study" of the broader principles mastered before reaching this stage. Of particular interest are worlds in trouble—where something in the structure and operation of the system has gone awry, where the creatures involved are maladapted to their circumstances. We trust we need not offer copious evidence that this is the condition of your planet now, ravaged by a mercurial experimental species (this means you).

You have been so conditioned to think of yourselves as the pinnacle of evolution—or as God's chosen species—that you lose sight of how brief your time on the planet has been, how ill-adapted you are to earthly life in many ways, and how rarely you operate from your exalted reason and much more often from irrational motive such as emotion and mythology. There is no other creature on the planet so poorly designed to withstand the rigors of your environs—while every other creature is encased in protective fur or feathers or scales, you stand naked and vulnerable before the wind, the rain, the sun, thorns and insects. What other creature sports such tender, vulnerable skin on its feet? Your eyesight, your hearing, your sense of smell, are but a dim fraction of the sensory powers of "lower" species.

Now, we are not trying to foster a species-wide inferiority complex. There is a reason for your weak and vulnerable design: it forces development of reason. With your powers of thought, memory, discernment, and speech, you are able to forge social alliances and manipulate the environment in ways no other species can match. You can fashion clothing and footwear to house your tender nakedness, agriculture to release you from constant foraging, machines to carry your burdens for you. Reason—not your maladapted bodies—makes you the masters of the planet.

And yet you are far more than your rational minds. You are deeply spiritual creatures, immersed in myth and fairy tale, inspired to altruism and savagery by religious beliefs lacking a whit of rational foundation. You are emotional beings, moved to tears and sacrifice and war by the mercurial swirl of emotions running roughshod over reason in their all-consuming intensity. You are psychologically complex, your minds a dissonant chorus of clashing voices, desires, and impulses.

So this experimental species—capable of love and barbarity, art and devastation, reason and madness, truth and deception—stands at a crucial juncture now, struggling to synthesize its conflicting intellectual, spiritual, emotional, and psychological aspects into a unified, integrated mind-field; a suprahuman consciousness. If it succeeds, the result will be a race which is truly the master of the planet—and with humility takes its proper place in the natural world that sustains it.

Because this transition is so critical, and its outcome so uncertain, this era has seen an unprecedented intervention by zeta-level entities into the earth sphere in the form of "channeled" entities. Desperate times call for urgent measures. The intention is to "tip the scales" in favor of accelerating the species' struggle toward holism and humility, and thus to avert eco-suicide. We should note that not all "entities" speak from the zeta level—some originate no further than a corner of the channel's mind—and due to the distance from earthly affairs, their perception is not always accurate. Probabilities blur together, and the daily routines and mechanics of earthly life are but dim memories. Still, the desire is to offer information which may help accelerate the species' struggle toward realization of its evolutionary potential—and avoid disaster.

Beyond the Zeta

As mentioned, there are virtually infinite gradations of consciousness beyond the zeta level, ever-expanding entities of increasing complexity, their mass-minds mastering ever more complex and abstruse aspects of reality. The goal of all life, all consciousness, is ultimately to return to the source, the Universal Mind, and contribute one's store of learning gathered along the journey.

Each of you, in your private life, is driven by this fundamental ambition—to live and prosper, realize your highest potential, gather diverse experience, leave your mark on the world. In doing so you take the first steps on a journey of unimaginable expanse and depth, from the earth plane to the astral plane, through the spiritual hierarchy, to the Universal Mind.

Happy trails!

4

Savages and Starbabies:
Soul Patterns of the New Generation

The news media are filled with stories of violent, almost feral, young people brutally assaulting each other, their parents, their teachers, their world, in paroxysms of mindless savagery rarely seen in prior generations. Less well noticed and publicized is the presence of a counterpoint to these amoral warriors, a stratum of young people carrying the perennial wisdom at the root of their consciousness, bringing a wisdom, a sensitivity, a holism to their engagement with the world, that has likewise rarely been seen in prior generations. Why the dichotomy between these emerging clusters of young people—savages and starbabies—and what is the overarching design lying behind their appearance?

Soul Clusters

We have written elsewhere[*] about the fields of consciousness from which individual souls spring. Briefly, the soul animating a human body is an offshoot of a "higher self" which contains the soul-offshoots of all earthly incarnations. In turn, the higher self is embedded within a still larger family of consciousness whose unique slant or focus of consciousness contributes to the diversity and stability of human culture. It is most accurate to visualize such relationships not as an organizational chart—with larger bodies of consciousness standing above and apart from smaller units—but as nested spheres, with each level of consciousness embedded within still greater fields.

There are no barriers or boundaries within the realm of pure consciousness, no restrictions on association. Where pools of

---

[*] See *Earthly Cycles.*

consciousness form, they do so based on natural sympathies, as like attracts like. All the offshoots of a given family of consciousness cluster together because it is most natural for them to do so. There are other natural clusters of association arising as well, which often cross "family" lines. For instance, all the souls born within a given age carry a natural sympathy because they are embarking on a common experience: earthly incarnation as a single generation. Another natural association is among souls incarnating in particular regions: all Americans, Swedes, Peruvians, Japanese, and Somalians enjoy a common bond for sharing a language, culture, and geography. A given soul, a given higher self, carries many such associations simultaneously, just as you may belong to a number of organizations with which you share common values and purpose.

The astral level is the "way station" between souls heading toward or returning from incarnation and physically based experience. The vibrational frequency of the astral level is sufficiently decelerated that consciousness at that level may "peer into" earth events to determine what is happening where. This aids in choosing a birth mother—the springboard for experiencing a specific cultural framework—on an individual soul level. At a higher level, guides from higher strata assist in assembling and preparing the souls of a common generation for their experience as brothers and sisters of a given age. These higher guides examine the current conditions on Earth, observe the trends most likely (but never fated) to unfold, and educate souls seeking birth about their likely experiences in a given age.

It may be that a soul being so apprised decides it would not be fruitful to incarnate at a given time. An old soul seeking a quiescent lifetime of minimal strife to "wrap up" a few loose ends would not find fulfillment in an age of social chaos and cultural breakdown. Conversely, a young Agitator soul eager to wreak havoc and ridicule on a staid culture would do well to avoid eras of such institutional repression that any budding agitator is quickly squelched—on the rack if necessary. There must be at least some potential for fulfillment of life purpose for a soul to choose incarnation in a given age.

Ask yourself what the higher guides, peering down at the events of the seventies, eighties, and nineties, might have to say to souls seeking incarnation in the last several decades. What sort of world would they be born into? Which life purposes could potentially find fulfillment within this milieu? What larger trends would such souls expect to play a part in? What would you say to a soul asking what the world was like, what it could expect to experience over the 60 or 80 years to come?

The Age of Polarization

It is apparent to any reasonably conscious person that yours is an age of turmoil and transformation. Surrounding you is the evidence of a culture fragmenting as its foundation crumbles beneath it. The power of the church, respect for government, faith in technology, the cohesion of the family, economic security—all these are crumbling, are they not? And looming above all societal concerns is the greater ecological crisis, portending degradation or collapse of the natural systems and processes on which humanity, and all species, depend.

All this is the natural and inevitable result of founding a culture on the core value of *separation*. This core value underlies your political, economic, religious, and technological systems. As it must, it can lead only to fragmentation and dissolution of those very structures. Yet these systems still wield enormous power, and their prized offspring of democratic capitalism now spreads across the Earth, embraced by nations eager for the wealth and comfort of a First World lifestyle.

At the same time, a new consciousness settles upon the globe, a consciousness imbued with a new cultural premise: holism. Working more in obscurity than in direct opposition to the prevailing cultural powers, the holistic worldview sprouts roots in the dust of the crumbling separatist worldview. In politics, in economics, in spirituality, in technology, the holistic paradigm offers an alternative, a new way of seeing and thinking and being in the world.

As the old culture's decline accelerates, those clinging to its values, and profiting from its success, naturally react with fear, struggling to shore up its crumbling foundation. Reactionary cries thunder through the social conversation, with calls for "back to basics" education, "family values," and chastity until marriage leading the charge backward toward an erstwhile stable, orderly society.

This, then, is the setup for the current era and the decades to come: the "final showdown" between the old separatist order and the new holistic worldview. The outcome is not in doubt; the separatist culture must collapse under the weight of its own faulty premises, as did the Soviet Union. Humanity, if it learns its lessons, will embrace holism as the foundation of a self-sustaining, self-renewing culture in harmony with the natural world.

Who would choose to be born into such an age? Who would choose to slip into the amnesia of human incarnation, playing a part in the unfolding drama of polarization, collapse, and rebirth? Such an era is attractive to souls of many life purposes, given the inherent drama in which such lives are played. But an era of turmoil and transformation is of particular interest to two types of souls: primitive baby and young souls attracted by the scent of chaos and violence; and mature and old souls offering healing to a wounded, staggering world.

The Savages

In a stable culture whose strong families patiently mold their children into dutifully productive citizens, a baby soul seeking to experience tumult and violence is often stymied by cultural mores and conscience. In a declining culture, where families splinter and parents abandon their responsibilities, little stands in the way of a baby soul's thirst for raw conflict and violence. Where a critical mass of such malformed, amoral young people arises, the law of the jungle takes root, cultural values are scorned, and allegiance to peers holds supreme. This scenario breeds mindless violence, attracting baby souls seeking raw expression of desire and impulse without restraint of conscience or morality.

This is not to suggest that there is a rogue family of consciousness feeding its violently amoral souls into an otherwise stable society. In fact, the behavior of violent youngsters holds a mirror up to the culture that bred them and shouts: Hypocrites! This is the world you've given us! The paper in your books and magazines comes from murdered forests! An entire ecosystem was swept away to build your house and sterile lawn! The clothes you wear are sewn by virtual slaves, some of them small children! Your economy is a voracious monster devouring the planet to reward the few while billions starve! Your religion has tortured and murdered untold victims

through the ages! Every aspect of your culture is soaked with violence! *And you know all this and still you do not change!*

The violent young savages, then, are not a mutation on the body
politic, not an alien species thrust upon the world. They are mirrors
of the culture that created them. They force attention to the violence
that permeates every nook and cranny of your culture. They shock,
horrify, and repulse; they maim and kill younger and younger; they
trigger a frenzied search for the source of their brutality: *whatever it
takes to jar awake a culture slumbering in denial of the violence it
employs as it consumes the Earth.*

The Starbabies

The other soul cluster attracted to an era of turmoil and transformation is that on the "other side" from their violent brethren: the
starbabies carrying an accelerated consciousness suffused with the
promise of a healthy world founded on holism. These are the weav-
ers of the new order. The challenge they face, ironically, is that while
they hold the brightest promise for the future, there are few extant
cultural patterns through which they can express their evolved nature.
Baby souls find limitless opportunities for committing mindless
violence—for the culture is "set up" for such behavior—but where
are the enlightened, holistically minded souls to express themselves?

The result is a fairly high degree of frustration manifesting as
learning disabilities, attention deficit disorder, behavior problems,
and alienation. The starbabies are saying, "We can find no outlet for
our higher energies and yet we cannot force them into your systems."
The result is frustrated, chaotic energy spewing forth in physical and
mental spasms for want of appropriate outlets.

It should be noted that this is not true of all starbabies, yet there
is an undeniable rise in the incidence of children with learning
disabilities, ADHD, etc. Those who cannot adapt to extant cultural
patterns, who cannot force their accelerated energies into anachro-
nistic, old-order social structures, find themselves with no other outlet but the random, chaotic expulsion of their energies.

In adolescence, such starbabies often find their frustration so
intense that they simply abandon all hope of fitting themselves into
society in a meaningful way; instead they sprout purple hair, dis-
figure themselves with tattoos and pierced body parts, and scorn

academic and career achievement. If such young people look like mutations, that is their intent: to scream that their evolved spiritual natures cannot and will not be satisfied with the impoverished life path offered by mainstream culture; if this is the best the world has to offer, they will abandon it to develop their own alien species.

Of course not all starbabies exhibit the vivid frustration evinced by children with learning disabilities or pierced eyebrows. Some find that a few of the traditional avenues offer enough of an outlet for their accelerated energies that some satisfaction can be won by working within the mainstream. Young people tirelessly working on behalf of environmental protection and restoration, caring for the poor and sick, working with AIDS sufferers, or involvement with church youth groups, all find venues of expression within traditional culture. They have a nagging sense that this is not enough, that this tinkering around the edges of an earth-devouring, soul-deadening machine is insufficient to truly heal the world, but they prefer doing something to alienation.

So starbabies tend to fall into two categories: those so frustrated and alienated that they abandon all hope of meaningful participation in traditional culture; and those finding outlets for their energies within the mainstream while biding their time to make a more meaningful impact later. Both live with the deeply felt certainty that their society is deeply and irredeemably flawed, yet they lack a clear blueprint for transforming the world in accordance with their inchoate visions.

The Mainstream

We do not mean to suggest that all young people fall into the families of savages and starbabies. In fact, the majority of the younger generation falls squarely in the mainstream, accepting without qualm the cultural legacy of their parents. While this may seem surprising, given that the traditional way of life is ultimately suicidal, the fact is that *most souls incarnating in an age of turmoil and transformation choose to experience its chaos and upheaval directly, without special knowledge or insight.* They want chaos and turmoil to fall on their heads, as it were, instead of recognizing the deeper process at work.

If earthly life is intended as a medium of learning and growth, then the most powerful learning springs from direct experience: from the passion and heartache of romance, the frustrations and rewards of parenthood, the struggle to forge a successful career, the challenges of disease and disability and growing old. The more intensely these issues are experienced, the greater the soul's learning. As a result, starbabies and savages (or keen intellects coolly observing cultural turmoil) have a diminished experience, for their higher awareness cheats them of pure, raw, animal encounters with reality. When one anticipates looming events, and recognizes their deeper meaning as they unfold, the soul's direct learning is diminished.

If you are reading these words, coming as they do from an unorthodox source and offering a higher perspective, chances are you have experienced the frustration of trying to convince others that the world is on a path to certain destruction, that you must change the way you organize society, that there are better alternatives for living in harmony with natural principles. And you have been met with blank stares and shrugged shoulders: What are you talking about? Whatever goes wrong will be fixed by science and the government. They fix everything. What is there to worry about?

If you can set aside your anger and frustration at facing such willfully bovine ignorance, recognize that those who toddle along unconcerned with global warming, war psychosis, or economic inequality, do so *because that is precisely what their souls want them to do.* Their higher selves know as well as any prophet's what looms on the horizon if your course is not righted, but their incarnated offshoots are "tuned" to suppress any such awareness. They are here to *directly experience* an age of turmoil and transformation, not to philosophize about it; they must have famine and war and plagues and disease and cultural collapse; they must be swept up in the maelstrom and feel its brutal effects with every fiber of their being.

So the majority of the young generation follows in its forebears' footsteps, accepting without protest the life path laid out for them and dutifully plodding along it. This great mass resists the prophetic cries for cultural transformation and global healing. They roll along, flanked on either side by the brutality of the savages and the prophecy of the starbabies. When the savages so assault their sensibilities that they decide *something must be done*, they cock a receptive ear toward the starbabies.

It can take a shocking incident to arouse the mainstream from its slumber. In the aftermath of a high school mass murder or horrific act of terrorism, society at large is aroused and frantic, searching for answers and meaning in the tragedy. While the voices crying for vengeance and punishment shout the loudest, on the edges of the social conversation wiser voices may be heard, urging restraint and introspection: what could we have done to contribute to this? What social policies and practices are in place that encourage such a vicious eruption? Though never the dominant voices in a tragedy's aftermath, the wiser voices find resonance in some mainstream hearts, there to gently take root. As the horror subsides, wisdom may flower; and the mainstream shifts a notch or two toward the visions of the starbabies.

This is the seesaw dynamic of social change: a great mainstream army marching along familiar, well-worn cultural ruts; to one side a small band of savages mirroring, through their violent pathology, the culture's darker aspects; to the other side a chorus of starbabies urging evolution to a higher and deeper worldview. When the mainstream is sufficiently provoked and aroused by the pathology of the savages, they become receptive to the prophecies of the starbabies and gradually absorb their higher wisdom.

The challenge in your era is that for the first time in history, humanity threatens the ecological fabric on which your lives, and those of other species, depend. Damage to the natural world is more insidious and less obvious than the ravages of the savages; so by the time awareness of such degradation registers, it is often too late to repair the damage, and great calamity ensues. Who sees the ocean level rising fraction by fraction? Who notices the voices of the songbirds falling silent as their rain forest refuges are slashed and burned? Who observes the erratic weather patterns portending diminished food production? None but the starbabies notice and warn and urge remedial action while the mainstream plods on, oblivious until disaster crashes through the roof.

Bringing Up Starbaby

If young starbabies are the promise of the future, a cluster of souls whose accelerated consciousness perceives the cultural crisis and potential solutions, how can such children be encouraged to develop their intuitive nature while still functioning reasonably well in mainstream culture? While such questions may be of greatest interest to educators and parents of young children, even a brief encounter with a young person in which his perceptions and visions are validated by an adult can make the difference between despair and hope, between alienation and commitment. Here are some suggestions for encouraging the highest and truest expression of starbaby consciousness.

The first suggestion, a broad one which holds true for all children in all ages, is to offer them respect. The tendency for adults in any culture is (naturally) to squeeze a child's free-flowing spirit into extant cultural molds. This molding springs from love, from a desire that a child have as easy and trouble-free a life as possible; and certainly thinking and acting with the mainstream is the easiest way to live.

But truly wise adults take a different approach. Recognizing that each child is born with a unique personality and life agenda, they seek not so much to mold the child's spirit as to encourage its flowering. Respect, then, means accepting a child for the unique spark of divinity he represents; offering a diverse range of experience to encourage that spark's brightest glowing; and refraining from heavy-handed inculcation of old-order values. Respect means asking a child (though not literally), "Who are you and why are you here? How can I help you reach your highest potential?"

A good practice to get into, then, if you would be respectful friends with children, is to get into the habit of seeing them as teachers, and you the student, rather than vice versa. Recognizing that they bring unique soul qualities to the world, and have a consciousness more accelerated than yours, open yourself up to being educated by asking questions, probing the recesses of their psyches, drawing out the secrets of their souls. You do this by asking questions and simply nodding in reply to whatever they say. Any judgmental response may immediately slam the door closed on further revelations.

Consider: if a teenage child or acquaintance related to you his experiences on LSD, how would you react?

As an example of the disrespect well-meaning adults offer youngsters, there is an unfortunate tendency to squelch the aggressive nature of children, especially boys. Adults often snatch away toy guns and discourage children from playing with the theme of violence and death. This reveals a profound ignorance of childhood and its purposes, and a great disrespect toward the children involved. A primary purpose of childhood is to play with the grand themes of human life. Good guy, bad guy, doctor, teacher, parent—they play them all, and through their play come to know what feels natural for them, what resonates in their soul. Where such explorations are restricted by misguided adults, shame settles in the soul, shame for being a "bad boy" in wanting to explore the very theme on which his society rests.

This is one small example of the ways in which misguided adults deform the souls of children. An adult offering genuine respect to children offers only one proscription: that no one literally get hurt during their play.

One of the most powerful tools in raising starbabies is art. At any age, art is the marriage of spirit and matter, a hybrid token of the soul's revelations. The "brilliance" of a work of art depends on the depth of the artist's communion with spirit. Cutting-edge art is often offensive or confusing to the mainstream, plugging along in its traditional ruts. By encouraging artistic expression in children, their soul vitality is nourished and strengthened.

A careful balance must be struck between offering no guidance at all and providing just enough direction and help that the child's visions can be made tangible while true to their origin. Obviously, a coloring book and box of crayons won't satisfy a starbaby. Providing raw materials—clay, blocks of wood, paints and brushes, string, paper—then allowing the child to fashion them however he pleases, is the best approach.

The ultimate result is irrelevant. The average five-year-old starbaby will not produce works threatening Picasso's place in art history. It is the *process* that matters: learning to make inner visions tangible, and doing so in a safe and encouraging environment with the guidance of respectful adults. This process tells the child that his inner visions are valid and valued, that time and materials will be provided for their expression, and that adults appreciate the fruits of his labor. This sets the stage for much richer and more meaningful soul-expressions later in life.

The most powerful art form for expression of starbaby consciousness is music. Music is the body's way of immersing itself in vibrational patterns carrying the energies of distant people, times, and places. The conscious parent of a starbaby strives to fill the house with music from all eras and cultures, so the child's vibrational field can sample the energetic patterns leading up to the present. Music carries subtle information, cleverly disguised as catchy tunes and thundering symphonies, and the starbaby wants to soak up the musical knowledge of his culture's past and present. It is seemingly curious that many of today's young people prefer the music of the Beatles to that of their own age; for the Beatles were the premier expression of the energies of joy, affirmation, and love, and their songs validate and reinforce the higher frequencies of starbaby consciousness.

We have offered three techniques encouraging the accelerated consciousness of starbabies. Offer them respect and allowance. Talk with them, ask them questions, elicit their deepest wisdom. Encourage artistic expression. There are many other techniques which wise and respectful adults use in encouraging children's soul growth, but the point is made: Because starbabies' consciousness is so accelerated, care must be taken that their highest potential be cherished and encouraged lest they collapse in frustration and alienation. For from such young people will arise the new order, the vaunted New Age, for which the weary world yearns.

5

Exploring the Brain:
Gatekeeper of Your Reality

The traditional scientific view of the brain is that it is the creator of all experience, all thought, all sensation: the very font of consciousness. Given that the notion of consciousness untethered to form is rejected by the scientific worldview, the belief that the brain is the source of all human thought and experience is ineluctable. It is also, however, limited and incomplete; for the brain is not the *creator* of experience, but the *mediator* of experience. It serves as the nexus between physical and nonphysical realms, between earthbound experience and higher realms of consciousness. Let us explore the brain and its miraculous workings, the better to restore it to its proper place in the creation of your experience.

The Gray Filter

The primary function of the brain is to *filter information*. As the mediator between physical and nonphysical realms, in every moment the brain is bombarded with neuronal impulses rising from the body, as well as swarms of information streaming from the higher realms. The brain's primary purpose is to sift through these raging rivers of information and sort them appropriately: what can be handled subconsciously; what can be ignored; what should be retained for future action; and what must be presented immediately to the conscious mind. Let us look at this more closely.

Waking consciousness is a state of outward-directed awareness in which the body receives information from, and acts upon, the material world. The body spends about two-thirds of each day in a state of fluctuating outer-awareness. During this time the body's needs for food, shelter, clothing, and rest must be met; relationships renewed through words and touch; plans for the future contemplated, discussed, and implemented. In other words, the body must be cared for, the circle of family and friends embraced anew, and one's place in the world confirmed.

Obviously, for such an outward-directed state to be maintained, information streaming from the higher realms must be suppressed. As well, most of the lower body's functions can proceed without conscious awareness; for there can be only so much information presented to the conscious mind at any time. Think of the conscious mind as a jar and each neuronal impulse as a grain of sand. The jar can hold only so much sand. When new grains demand admission, other grains must first be removed.

The conscious mind always holds a blend of externally originating impulses (a picture of the physical world woven by the senses) and streams of thought descending from higher levels of consciousness. Because maintaining focus on the external world is more of a "strain" than inner reverie, the relative proportion of inner and outer impulses determines the quality of waking consciousness. When the focus is entirely external—as in an emergency—the brain maintains a sharp, intense focus on earthly experience; in quiescent environs, the higher orders of thought and contemplation waft to the fore (monks and mystics retreat to caves and monasteries for this reason).

The brain's job is to mediate this dynamic flux between inner and outer worlds, sifting their flows of impulse to maintain a seemingly consistent out-picture of the physical world and a continuity of thought while operating within it. The brain allows enough information about the external world to ensure the body's awareness of its environs and security within them; only when bodily security is ensured are higher flows of thought granted awareness. The brain fills the jar of conscious awareness from the bottom up: first all essential information from the body and external world is projected into awareness; what space remains in the jar is granted to higher thought.

How does the brain decide which information is crucial, which is of moderate importance, and which is irrelevant? There are two sources of such information: certain hardwired "templates" built into the brain's structure, and a larger field of knowledge carried in the energy fields encircling the body. The templates are universal, species-wide reactions to specific stimuli portending pleasure or pain. When such stimuli are perceived by the senses, the brain matches them with their templates in its " template library" and reacts accordingly. The roaring crash of a tree, the sting of burning skin, the amorous touch of a lover—all these trigger universal reactions of embrace or flight. In the case of great danger, there is no time for contemplation: impulses toward flight are immediately triggered, without the higher regions of the brain even considering the wisdom of such a course.

Beyond these hardwired templates, decisions as to whether stimuli are to be presented to the conscious mind are made by a more elaborate and sophisticated process involving the energy fields surrounding the body. For here is where the higher self has imprinted its intentions for a lifetime upon the body; here the relative importance of various stimuli are sculpted into vitality. Stimuli rising from the senses which don't match any hardwired template are passed on to the upper part of the brain, the cerebrum, which serves as the nexus between the physical and higher bodies. In a process difficult to describe, the cerebrum serves as a "screen" on which sensory impulses are projected, while a layer of energy floating just above the cerebrum scans the projected impulses for their relative importance. Where a powerful "match" is found, the sensory impulse is stimulated by a burst of accelerated energy, which alerts the brain that it is to include the impulse in its constantly updated picture of conscious awareness.

Consider an example: the higher self has chosen the theme "poverty-wealth" for a given lifetime, and has imprinted that theme into the energy fields encircling your body. As you walk down the street, you are constantly bombarded with stimuli, most of which are discarded as irrelevant to both bodily safety and your life theme. But images dense with "poverty" and "wealth" will trigger resonant impulses in the higher fields—for this is the chosen life theme—and will be pressed into conscious awareness. "Look at that poor, starving homeless person," you think; or "Look at that disgusting display of ostentatious wealth." Other people swirling around you hardly notice what rivets your attention; for their life themes lie elsewhere.

How does the brain create its dynamically flowing stream of conscious awareness? What does it mean to be awake and aware?

While it may seem as though an impermeable wall separates sleep from wakefulness, in fact they gradually shade into each other. The primary difference, of course, is that in wakefulness one's attention is focused outward onto the physical world, while in sleep attention shifts to the higher realms of consciousness. To again use the metaphor of a jar, in wakefulness the jar is largely filled with externally originating grains of stimuli while in sleep the grains flow from above with just a scant few of external source. At some hazy point, where the balance between outer and inner worlds shifts, one is considered to have "fallen asleep."

Wakefulness is actually an artificial state; for in deepest terms the physical world is an illusion, a projection of consciousness of seeming substance and durability. One's authentic, natural state is of pure consciousness. Where consciousness projects itself into a physical medium and seeks growth through experience within that medium, it is forced to operate through processes foreign to the native qualities of consciousness. Thus it is a "strain" to operate within the physical world, and that strain can be sustained for only so long before it must be relieved by restoration to a state of pure consciousness, as in sleep.

Wakefulness is sustained by adjusting the brain's filtering process to favor externally originating information. Imagine the brain as a gatekeeper standing watch between two opposite gates. When one gate opens by a certain degree, the opposite gate must close by the same measure, so their combined angles are always equal. To create wakefulness, the brain opens wide the gate to the physical world, while commensurately closing the gate to the higher realms. This forces the brain to deal largely with external stimuli; intention is focused on engaging with and manipulating physical reality. At the same time, a subtle but steady "identity foundation" must flow from the energy fields, giving a name, history, and life theme to the body it animates. You must know who you are and what you want if you are to act consistently and purposefully in the physical world.

Wakefulness is a strain because the physical world vibrates at a much slower frequency than pure consciousness. Consciousness must "step down" many levels of frequency in order to manipulate within the physical world. Imagine talking v-e-r-y s-l-o-w-l-y all day so that a foreigner could understand you. You would quickly tire of the strain of speaking slower than your natural pace. The same holds true for consciousness, decelerating to operate within the physical realm.

It is the brain that suffers the strain in this process, for it must mediate between bodily impulse and pure consciousness. Being a physical organ, it naturally vibrates at the level of matter, yet it constantly interacts with highly accelerated vibrational fields, particularly the field nestled against the cerebrum. Such strain is unsustainable; thus the body must "switch out" of the artificial wakeful state for one-third of every day, allowing the brain to recover and prepare for another day's adventures.

Brain and Body

Given the materialistic perspective of modern science, it is natural to assume that all of the body's various functions and processes are regulated by the brain through hormonal and biochemical messengers. Response to injury, maintenance of internal rhythms like the menstrual cycle, and sensory receptors, all appear to have specific governing sites within the brain and to be mediated by biochemical processes. All this is true, but the picture is incomplete. Let us sketch it a bit more broadly.

The physical body is but the densest of the cocooned energy bodies forming the greater physical self. Among the unseen fields encircling the body is its energetic double, its nonphysical twin. This twin is not a precise replica of the body at any specific stage of life; rather, it contains all probable expressions of the body from conception to death. It might be thought of as the probable body, a body of infinite potential, of which the physical body reflects just a sliver in any moment.

You know that the raw materials of the body are continuously replaced over a span of seconds, hours, days, or years; yet the body remains uniquely you even as it grows and matures. How is form held constant amid the constant flushing and rebuilding of the body? Through the probable—twin—body.

Imagine a minute strand of light binding each cell of the probable body with its physical twin. Along this strand flow vitalizing instructions to each physical cell; and, in response, an apprisal of the cell's status. The probable body, through this exchange, regulates growth and development, maturity and aging. It instructs the cells of the budding embryo whether they are brain, skin, muscle, bone, or organ. It triggers the onset of puberty, oversees the mellowing of youth's vigor to the industry of middle age, then to the quiescence of old age. When so instructed by the higher self, it shuts off the flow of life-sustaining energy, beginning the death process.

Where is the brain in all of this? For the most part it is simply taking orders. When the probable body instructs that puberty should be launched, the brain stimulates the hypothalamus, which triggers a hormonal flood throughout the body. The brain does not decide when puberty should begin; it simply processes the decision once it has been made; its job is to regulate the process and ensure its smooth fulfillment. The brain itself undergoes massive changes during puberty, promoting the psychological flowering from childhood's insular self-absorption to youth's global passion.

The relationship between probable body and the brain might be compared to that between the president of a company and its floor managers. The president sets the overall course and tone of the business; the floor managers handle the many minute details required to manifest the president's vision. So the probable body sets the overall look and dimensions of the body, schedules its growth and maturity, and implements death when so advised by the higher self. The brain implements these broad plans with the precise, intricate, multifarious processes involved in keeping the body alive, healthy, and on the maturational schedule dictated by the probable body.

The brain also apprises the probable body anytime something out of the ordinary occurs. This happens automatically as any unusual condition—such as a sudden mobilization of the immune system in response to injury—generates frequencies perceived by the probable body. Anytime the brain goes on alert, the probable body is instantly apprised of the situation as the brain generates "crisis" frequencies. While the brain is entrusted with immediate handling of the situation, any long-term, chronic condition would also be mediated by the probable body as it tries to restore health to the body. Again, the brain's repertoire is rather limited to "first aid" responses, while the larger healing process is mediated by the probable body.

Anatomy of the Brain

The brain is divided into regions specializing in various discrete tasks and processes. Let us explore the brain with an eye not only to anatomy but also to the higher energetic bodies with which the brain works so intimately.

The brain has distinct regions called the brain stem, the cerebellum, and the cerebrum. The brain stem is the most primitive area of the brain, controlling basic physiological processes: pleasure and pain, hunger and thirst, the sex drive, and so on. Most of the brain stem's activities take place beneath conscious awareness. The cerebellum, nestled behind the brain stem, controls balance and coordination. The cerebrum, the uppermost layer of the brain, is where human thought and artistry reside.

The cerebrum is cleaved into right and left hemispheres. In general the use of language and logic is centered in the left hemisphere, while the right hemisphere mediates artistic ability and spatial visualization. The two hemispheres communicate through a bundle of nerve fibers called the corpus callosum.

This is the map of the brain as drawn by modern science and it is valid as far as it goes. It is true that discrete regions of the brain specialize in mediating various functions and processes. What is missing from this picture, however, is the recognition that the brain itself is, in turn, mediated and directed by still higher fields of energy. In other words, the brain is not the ultimate arbiter and creator of experience, but is one link in the chain of processes through which experience is created.

As with the rest of the body, the brain has a duplicate twin within the probable body. It is through the probable brain that the higher self sculpts its intentions for the experience to be gained in a lifetime. Removed from the skull, all brains look pretty much alike: the brain of a mass murderer is indistinguishable from that of a saint. What can account for the stark contrast in behavior? The answer lies not in the physical brain but in the probable brain.

Each region of the brain hums at a distinct frequency and with certain signature patterns. This specialization is what allows for differences in thought and behavior, for the probable brain can stimulate certain areas while suppressing others. The probable brain, which encases and permeates the physical brain, emits frequencies to stimulate various regions of the physical brain. Through "mixing and matching" the suppression and stimulation of various regions of the brain, the probable brain enforces the higher self's intention for the psychological framework of waking consciousness.

Almost everyone is granted a full and unrestricted flow of stimulating energy to the brain stem and cerebellum. After all, these regulate largely unconscious processes necessary for survival. It is in the higher brain centers, the cerebral hemispheres, that a more precise and sophisticated blend of stimulating and suppressing energies stamps the template of personality onto the brain and body.

As an example, think of the broad continuum of human sexual behaviors. Everything from long-term monogamy to one-night stands to rape lies along this continuum: from the most sublime expression of lifelong love and commitment to the brutal violation of another's body. The originating impulse in the brain stem is identical in all cases: "We want sex now." What moderates this broad, diffuse, imperious urge? The cerebrum, where lies all morality. The probable brain, stimulating the physical brain with lesser or greater flows to the "morality" regions of the cerebrum, moderates the brain stem's urgent desire: insisting that it be fulfilled in a loving, mutually fulfilling encounter; allowing some leeway, some duplicitous smooth talk to land a one-night stand; or placing no restrictions at all, even on the brutal taking of another. The strength of the moderating stimulation from the probable brain determines the extent to which a brain stem impulse will be directed toward socially validated expression. (Of course, childhood experience of love and affection informs this process as well.)

This is how the various soul ages are imprinted onto the brain and body. A baby soul is virtually unhindered by moral inhibitions, meaning the probable brain emits only enough stimulation to the cerebrum to ensure that one's socially unacceptable violations are hidden from view. If sex reflects, in deepest terms, the desire to incorporate another's essence—to transcend the isolated ego by forging an integrated, transpersonal gestalt of energy—then a baby soul may murder and cannibalize his "partners," since there is no stimulation to the cerebrum telling him not to. However repugnant, it is a logical way of fulfilling the brain stem's impulses toward sexual union and incorporation with others.

A young soul receives more guiding stimulation from the probable brain, leavening brain-stem impulses with recognition of its culture's moral code. A young soul may try to "work around" that code, paying it just enough heed to remain within the boundaries of social approbation. The eternal hustler and charmer of women, whose love life is sprinkled with brief, torrid romances and one-night encounters, is a young soul whose moral center receives just enough stimulation that he at least acknowledges the ideal of long-term commitment even as he has no intention of realizing that ideal. Young souls play by the rules even as they try to squirm around them in search of immediate gratification.

Mature souls enjoy a full, rich flow of stimulation from the probable brain to the cerebrum's moral center. In fact, their morality is so deep and timeless that it frequently clashes with their culture's moral code. Theirs is a universal morality rooted in respect and allowance for all beings; it cares little for the shifting legal proscriptions of younger souls legislating their restrictive moral codes. Sex, to a mature soul, is a rich, warm exchange with another who is cherished first as a unique and precious soul, and only secondarily as a source of sensual pleasure.

Old souls enjoy what might be called "complete sympathy" between probable and physical brains; that is, the probable brain no longer mediates its flow through selective stimulation and suppression. As the probable brain receives impulses from higher fields, it stands with floodgates wide open, feeding an unmediated flow to the physical brain. Thus the old soul's morality is even more timeless and universal than the mature soul's. The old soul does not clash with the cultural proscriptions of its day; it simply ignores them as irrelevant. Suffused with an eternal wisdom of the ages, the old soul's cerebrum smothers any brain-stem impulse under a blanket of timeless morality. Sex is frequently abandoned altogether by old souls, for they recognize the oneness of all creation and feel no need to "incorporate" the essence of others who, they recognize, are already carried within themselves.

This process of variable energetic flows stimulating the physical brain carries into all other aspects of human personality and ability. Where artistic talent is desired by the higher self, the probable brain offers high stimulation to the right cerebral hemisphere, as well as to the regions of the brain governing the particular talent sought: visual artistry, musical talent, writing skill. By manipulating a number of such energetic flows, the probable brain can govern both the quality of artistry and its particular medium of expression.

The impulse toward artistic expression is, at base, a desire to plunge into the spiritual realms and to fashion the insights gained there into symbolic fragments; then to share these metaphorical insights with the larger culture. Thus the probable brain acts as a gatekeeper between the physical brain and the higher spiritual realms. Where little artistic talent is desired by the higher self, the probable brain offers little stimulation, little access to the higher realms, forcing attention on the gross material world. Where true artistry is sought, the probable brain "opens the gate" to the upper realms, allowing an unhindered flow of spiritual energy to the cerebrum, which in turn sparks the urge toward artistic creation. Obviously, the flow can be adjusted to produce anything from mild "pop" talent to thundering genius.

We have used the examples of soul age and artistic talent to underscore that the brain is not the ultimate creator of personality and experience; rather, it is the handmaiden of the probable brain and the higher self, which determine personality and earthly experience by stimulating or suppressing various regions of the brain. The brain is like a computer, albeit an extraordinarily complex one, in that it faithfully carries out the programming imposed from without.

Brain and Spirit

As we have discussed, the waking brain's principal function is keeping the body safe, navigating it through the material world. Yet the brain also supports philosophical musing, ethical ideals, future projection, and spiritual longing. How can the same gray matter regulating such mundane functions as heartbeat and blood pressure soar to the lofty heights of spiritual and philosophical abstraction?

If there is one characteristic distinguishing humanity from other species, it is this quality of higher thought, and the yearning for spiritual perfection. There is no qualitative difference in the neurons processing bodily functions or enlightenment; the difference lies in the probable brain and its interaction with the physical brain. Humanity is unique in that it is given a maladapted body for the planet on which it lives, which forces creative adaptation and use of tools and materials to fashion shelter and clothing, acquire food, and so on. This requires a region of the probable brain devoted to intellect, to decision making, to creativity, to projecting the consequences of actions: in short, human thought.

Once such a region was established, it opened the doorway to still more refined and abstract uses of thought. It was decided, in establishing the parameters of human life, that a few strands of the probable brain's flow would offer a higher, more refined quality of energy allowing the highest levels of abstract thought—the realm of philosophy and the spirit. Questions such as, who am I? why am I here? where do we come from? what is the meaning of life? would be triggered by these strands of what might be called contemplative thought.

As with every other quality, the relative intensity of contemplative thought varies from individual to individual as part of the higher self's template for each lifetime. Baby souls, whose energy is focused at the brain stem with little stimulation at the cerebrum, care nothing for such questions, while old souls care about little else.

What is curious is that, while individuals blessed with powerful spiritual flows are relatively rare, almost everyone feels some spiritual urgings and a desire to answer the gnawing Ultimate Questions. Although the brain devotes a minute fraction of its energy to contemplating such issues, they rise in prominence because they are so much more compelling than the humdrum mechanics of the brain stem. Once the door is opened, however slightly, to realms of the spirit, even those few slender strands pulsing from the probable brain are enough to trigger at least a modicum of spiritual longing in the heart of every person. Also, whether conscious or not, you all know you will someday die, and you burn with curiosity—if not fear—to know what lies beyond the veil.

It is not intended that every person realize enlightenment; in fact, such would contradict the purpose of earthly life, which is to navigate through the facade of a material world. The spiritual realm is meant to be kept largely out of sight. As a result, but a tiny region of the brain is receptive to the ethereal stimulations of the probable brain—just enough to allow for contemplation of the Ultimate Questions while blocking access to the Ultimate Answers. If you were enlightened, you would not need to be in flesh. So spirit and brain join in allowing an occasional peek behind the illusory curtains of material existence, a glimpse of the deeper realities whirring beneath your everyday experience, the better to enrich your earthly journey.

In closing, while in the mainstream view the brain is the ultimate creator of experience, in fact it is the mediator of experience, the nexus between physical and spiritual realms, one link in a chain of processes creating your earthly experience. This in no way diminishes its extraordinary capacities and super-efficient processing of vast swarms of information. Rather, we hope to paint a grander picture of your being, one in which brain and body are enveloped in ever-expanding fields of energy and consciousness. The brain is diminished in such a picture only because your true reality is so much grander than a three-pound globe of neurons. Think about it!

6

The Unquiet Dead:
Visitations from Beyond the Veil

The world's mythology and literature are haunted by spectral visitors from "the other side," ectoplasmic intruders aiding, warning, guiding, and terrorizing humankind. Every culture, from the aboriginal to the wired, spins tales of vaporous apparitions, of a constant commerce across the permeable boundary dividing souls freed of flesh from those still encased within it. If death silences the lips, whence arises the ceaseless clamor from beyond the veil?

Swimming in Gelatin

Your senses deceive you. They convince you that you live in a world of rock, water, and air; and that living creatures draw upon these three basic elements to form their bodies. As modern physics confirms, the various densities of matter you perceive are in truth swirling fields of vibration governed by principles of attraction and resistance. Attraction means stability; resistance means chaos. Let us briefly review the vibrational fields germane to earthly life.*

The rocks and soil beneath your feet are not hard and dead and static; they are pulsating vibrational fields, densely packed and relatively quiescent so as to appear solid and stable over time. Their "cells" are drawn together in a fierce embrace of attraction. Water is a much more dynamic field of vibration, suffused with the vigorous dance of attraction and resistance among its vibrational cells. And air—that blanket of atmosphere enveloping you with life-giving oxygen—appears entirely empty; only a cooling breeze or fierce wind hints at the swarms of high-velocity energy which escape your senses, driven by a fierce dance of resistance.

Rather than moving through an "empty" atmosphere of air, it is more accurate to say you are swimming in gelatin. That is, air plays

---
* See *Conscious Life* for a more comprehensive discussion.

host to highly energized particles swirling in unstable, dynamically shifting fields of vibration knowing much more resistance than attraction. This has several effects. One is that it allows life to flourish. Because bedrock, soil, and any durable substance, including the foods you ingest, are heavily skewed toward "attraction," they provide the stability and consistency physical beings require to survive. Yet without the stimulative influence of air—that madly swirling dance of resistance—your body and those of all other beings would soon slow to the deadly static pulse of bedrock.

There can be only so much of a "gap" between the vibrational frequencies of a substance and the consciousness that animates it. A stone cannot ponder the meaning of its existence. It is conscious, yes, in its way, but in a dreamy, quiescent slumber akin to coma. To "lighten up" the bodies of animate creatures, they must regularly ingest the fiercely dynamic fields of resistance swirling in air; this invigorates the body, stimulating the bedrock elements to greater dynamism than is their natural state, keeping the body limber and supple and swift. In turn, the body's dynamic vibrational fields allow a higher, more complex consciousness to animate it; to reach the lofty realms of human self-awareness, intellectual prowess, and artistic expression.

We offer a new word for this gelatinous field of vibration you call air: gelair. By coining a word we avoid having to use familiar words in unfamiliar meanings. Gelair is the seemingly empty and invisible field floating above bedrock, host to a crackling swirl of resistance essential for living creatures to balance the static pull of bedrock.

Going Astral

Death is a sequential process, of which only the first step is apparent on the earthly plane. The consciousness animating a body departs, leaving a decaying corpse behind. This is how you define death. But there are many steps beyond this initial liberation of the soul. It does not instantly shuck off the trappings and habits of physical existence, but gradually releases them as it rises through a series of increasingly rarefied etheric fields. These fields are not literally tiered in ascending levels toward some distant heaven; all fields overlap and interpenetrate. The vibrational quality of one's consciousness determines which field one "finds oneself in" and can competently manipulate within; the other fields—though swirling all around—are "invisible," being of higher or lower densities.

The first field beyond the physical is the astral field. The astral field is one vibrational step away from gelair. Because it does not play host to bedrock-based creatures, it is relatively free of the dance of attraction and resistance which suffuses the grosser physical level. There is, however, enough of a vibrational sympathy that some of the "waves" of resistance and attraction wash through the astral field, creating an attenuated replica of the physical field. This provides a degree of comfort and familiarity to souls departing the physical level; they find their reflexive ways of operating still hold to a limited extent. Because the astral field is a "way station" both for souls preparing to leap into physical life and those releasing it, its faint ambiance of attraction and resistance offers a gentle "bath" resonant of the energies of physical life.

You may be familiar with the common experience of near-death survivors: the ascent through a tunnel toward a bright light, being met by deceased loved ones or religious figures, feeling suffused with ineffable love and acceptance. Most of what the soul encounters immediately following physical death is a hallucination, conjured up by both the transitioning soul and its guiding spirits. The soul "fools itself" into carrying its sensory perception into the astral field, though there are no bedrock objects perceptible to touch, sight, and sound.

A soul's attachment to earthly life and willingness to release it determine how long it persists in operating through earthbound sensory processing. A sudden death, particularly where the body is severely mangled, can propel a soul to the astral level with such force that some time passes before the soul even realizes it is no longer in a physical body; it simply thinks it is dreaming. Dying in old age with a lifetime of regrets, of bitter grudges zealously nurtured, of thoughtless insults and abuse hurled at loved ones, may leave a soul reluctant to release the earth plane for it wishes to set right its many wrongs, to avoid the inescapable karmic imperative. Souls having lived good, decent, honest lives and consciously participating in the dying process are much more likely to accept their condition and to shed the artificial crutches of the senses once arrived at the astral plane.

One is bound to the astral plane until one has fully understood and accepted the fact of physical death, understands the process through which one will now proceed as mediated by spirit guides, and has released the dependence on sensory processing. A soul accepting its situation and eager for spiritual growth will move beyond the astral plane to higher realms. Those souls unable or unwilling to understand their situation, to accept it, and to embrace the spiritual path, will remain at the astral level. It is here, at the astral level, that the legions of ghostly visitors to the Earth reside.

Seeping Through the Cracks

We must resort to metaphor when describing the structure of gelair and the astral plane, as there is no precise parallel in your experience. Gelair's structure, while highly dynamic and unstable, nonetheless has a relatively uniform consistency (as does gelatin). It is a blanket of vibration encircling the Earth.

Just as the Earth's bedrock crust is a solid, dense series of layers, here and there riddled with faults and fissures, so are there "cracks" in gelair's otherwise homogenous consistency. Like lightning rods, these fissures are capable of channeling energy of a much higher frequency than gelair itself. Through these fissures, energy can travel from astral plane through gelair to bedrock, without the deceleration usually required for transmission from higher to lower fields. Highly accelerated energy can directly impinge on the bedrock level only where such fissures allow.

These fissures are often known as "power spots," areas of unusual electromagnetic activity, recognized by native peoples as sacred for the richness of the visions and prophecies received there. Often such fissures are linked with underground pockets of air, either caves or rock fissures, for the presence of gelair's frenzied dance of resistance beneath bedrock provides a link to highly accelerated astral-level energy. This is not always the case; there are many more fissures in the gelair layer than there are recognized power spots. Such fissures, like the veins and arteries of your body, range from wide "pipelines" to tiny threads.

As mentioned, what divides the earth level from the astral level is simply the difference in vibrational frequencies. They both occupy the same "space." One is bound to bedrock, the other floats above it.

The fissures between the planes allow a restricted flow of energy between them. The flow goes both ways: in the dream state or in heightened inspiration your consciousness may ascend a fissure into the astral level, there to swim in realms of experience unavailable to the earthbound. And the downward flow allows those souls on the astral level, under certain circumstances, to descend to their familiar earthly haunts.

Making a Specter of Oneself

Why would an astral-level soul wish to return to Earth? We have already mentioned a few possibilities: sudden death, keen regrets. Resolving unfinished business, bidding a final farewell to beloved ones, or checking up on spouse and children left behind, are several other motives for breaching the barrier. Especially unhappy souls, those stubbornly refusing to accept the fact of their physical demise, or those frightened by the prospect of spiritual growth and its attendant loss of egoic identity, return to the earth plane as escape from the inevitable. There is no timetable for the soul to complete its astral-level work and move on; complete freedom is granted every soul to progress at its desired pace. Some, faced with the choice, choose to duck tail and run back to the familiar. Their ability to do so, however, is severely limited by the vibrational disparity between earth and astral levels, and the constricted vibrational flow through gelair fissures.

The success or failure of an attempt to return to the earth plane depends on several factors. One is the nature of one's intent: is it simply to check up on those left behind, or is it a more direct intervention—making oneself visible to those in flesh, manipulating physical objects? Obviously, the former, merely returning to the earth plane for a scan of current events, is more easily conducted because it does not require manipulation of matter. Tom Sawyer is not the only one to attend his own funeral! Loved ones may feel a "presence," a subtle, featherlike brush of a familiar hand, as consolation from the departed to the grieving. It is fairly common for a departed soul to remain earthbound for a few days following death, keeping a foot in both realms as a way of easing its transition and sending consoling thoughts to its loved ones.

Direct physical manipulation is more difficult for a discarnate soul to achieve. Several conditions must be present: gelair fissures of sufficient breadth that they can transmit a strong flow of energy from the astral level; presence of magnetic "grounds," either inanimate objects or living beings, which anchor and amplify the astral energy; and a psychological openness on the part of those fleshbound souls participating in the experience. Let us look at these conditions in more detail.

Astral energy cannot simply be projected into the bedrock realm whenever and wherever an astral-level soul desires to make contact. Certain barriers are set up to minimize interdimensional contact; else your lives would be quickly taken over by swarms of souls eager to remain ensconced within their familiar earthly haunts. The presence of gelair fissures allows a limited opportunity for such contact, but the fissures constrict and attenuate the astral energy so that it does not overwhelm the denser physical realm, nor can its intrusion be widespread. Think of a dam holding back acres of water, with a few small cracks allowing a trickle of water to escape. This is the effect gelair fissures have on constraining the flow of astral energy to the earth plane.

Like lightning searching for a ground to anchor its supercharged energy, astral energy links most effectively with the earth plane when it anchors to a magnetic ground. Rather than the energy being diffused and dissipated in the atmosphere, a magnetic ground pulls astral energy in a clean, direct path to the Earth. Such magnetic grounds can be either inanimate objects or living beings. Rocks with a high metallic content, crystals, some hardwoods, and fabricated metals all serve as effective grounds. Possessed of a certain vibrational matrix, they easily absorb and anchor the compatible frequencies of astral energies.

Living beings, especially those offering powerful flows of dynamic energy, are also effective magnetic grounds. An organism in good physical and psychic health, and at a stable stage of life, is enveloped in an insular vibrational shell, not conducive to serving as an astral anchor. Unstable organisms, spewing excess or chaotic energy, serve as attractants to astral energy. Human adolescents are especially effective magnets for astral energy, with their dynamic sexual energies, rapid growth, and psychological instability. Those lying far outside the range of "normal" psychological stability—

geniuses, visionaries, artists, and psychopaths—more easily serve as astral anchors. Animals, particularly domesticated pets like cats and dogs, can be very effective anchors, for they too straddle human and nonhuman realms.

One of the rules governing interdimensional relations is that, while there must be allowance for some contact between physical and nonphysical realms, for the most part earthbound beings are to be left alone. Every culture weaves pantheons of gods and spirits and heavens and hells as recognition of the ephemeral nature of earthbound experience, beyond which lie greater realms of spirit. Nonetheless, it would not serve you well, while in flesh, to be constantly visited and guided and nagged by those in spirit; it would distract you from focusing on physical existence and gaining the experiences to be had only within its wondrously deceptive facade.

In order to make contact with the earthly realm, therefore, astral-level entities must seek permission to intrude. That permission may be consciously and openly granted, as with couples at a Ouija board; or it may arise subconsciously from a troubled, unstable, chaotic personality whose many psychic fissures and eruptions form "openings" through which astral entities can link with a host body as a magnetic ground.

We anticipate your objections. If we create our own reality, you say, how is it possible that an astral entity can simply dive into our energy fields without our conscious permission? The key word is *conscious*. Reality creation does not begin and end in the conscious mind; in fact, the vast majority of the processes through which you create your reality whir beneath the ego's awareness. When a person is troubled or unhappy, he or she is *always* looking for escape from misery, for new information, for some flash of insight that will end the suffering. Thus there is an openness to any source of inspiration or information; fissures are opened in the auric field to catch whatever tendrils of insight might float by. This is the "permission," expressed as vibrational fissures, an astral entity must find before it can link with a human body. (We will take up the subject of possession later.)

So astral energy must be grounded to earth before it can effectively operate within the physical realm. This grounding allows the astral entity to make itself aware of its environs, to detect the living and inanimate entities in its surroundings. In many cases this is all the astral entity desires: awareness of loved ones left behind without intervention.

In cases where direct intervention is desired, a more complex process is triggered. Here several conditions must be met before an intervention can be successful: the flow of astral energy must be sufficiently strong; multiple gelair fissures of adequate size must allow the flow of such energy; a powerful magnetic ground must anchor and amplify the energy; and, most important, no harm can befall any earthbound creature.

This last is particularly important. Karma can be incurred only by entities at the physical level, and must be resolved at the physical level. For an astral entity to cause deliberate physical harm to an earthbound being would violate this inviolable law. Any such intentions are "choked off" as energy flows through gelair fissures; energies imbued with the "intention to cause harm" are blocked. At best (or worst, depending on one's perspective), an astral entity may cause some *psychological distress* to an earthbound being, simply by manifesting itself or rattling doors. This is not direct physical harm, as a knife in the back would be, because the recipient of such harmless intervention can respond in any way he chooses, and can always shield himself from further disturbance by commanding the intrusive spirit to depart.

As you can see, a number of propitious circumstances must be present for an astral entity to make its presence known on the earth plane. The presence of gelair fissures and a magnetic ground are the bare minimum required, and a psychologically open or unstable host enhances the astral entity's ability to make contact.

In most cases an astral entity desires to make contact for a specific purpose which, once fulfilled, obviates the need for further contact. Making one's presence known to a beloved spouse or child; offering a crucially important piece of information; or simply satisfying oneself that the bereaved are overcoming their grief—once these intentions are fulfilled, the entity may return to the astral level to resume its spiritual journey.

A long-term presence is rarer for it is sustained by an entity seemingly incapable of coming to its astral senses, realizing where it is, recognizing that it no longer operates within the physical realm, and moving on with grace. Because freedom is the rule, astral entities may take as long as they wish—years, decades, centuries—to pursue their oblique intercourse with the physical realm. They may remain lodged in familiar houses or gardens, "protecting" them through the ages, not trusting any other earthbound being to properly care for them. They may even attempt to frighten current residents into abandoning their homes so the rightful owner—as the astral entity sees it—is restored as the master of the manor.

Taking Possession

We have mentioned that unstable personalities may serve as attractants for astral entities seeking an opening, a magnetic ground. What about full-bore possession, though, in which the body seems to be entirely taken over by a discarnate, often evil, personality?

We reaffirm that you create your own reality and that such possessions would never occur without the express—albeit unconscious—permission and acquiescence of the "possessed." Not only that, but much of the demonic behavior—shocking! blasphemous!—is instigated by the host "victim."

Again, no astral entity could completely take over a living being's body and use it for its own pleasure and benefit. In cases of genuine possession, where the possessed demonstrates strength and knowledge of which he is normally incapable, a pact is struck between possessed and astral entity. The terms of the pact are that the possessed appears to surrender its will and control over its body to the intruding spirit; the spirit uses the host's permission to manipulate within the physical realm, blending its energies with the host's to create superhuman strengths; while ultimate authority rests with the host. That is, no behavior is expressed without first passing through the filter of the host's mind, which retains ultimate authority.

Oftentimes possession is a mutually staged psychodrama in which the host liberates himself to express thoughts and feelings considered taboo within his family or culture. With all impulses toward such behavior blocked by convention, the host's psychological chaos may "invite" an astral entity looking for an earthly outlet. Together they stage a drama in which the host seems to relinquish all control over speech and behavior while the "evil" spirit takes over. Vulgar language, fascination with sexual and excretory functions, and religious blasphemy are all released in a torrent of long-suppressed energies suddenly liberated. The family is shocked and scandalized, of course, secretly delighting the host. The astral entity's energy amplifies the host's, resulting in superhuman strength, knowledge, or abilities the host alone does not possess.

Possession may dissipate on its own as the astral entity has its fill of naughty child's play or the host's long-repressed emotions are spent; or the psychodrama may continue unabated until an exorcism is staged. An exorcism is simply a mythodrama staged to counter the host's psychodrama. When the host feels helpless to express himself openly, when he feels unvalued and afraid and worthless, an exorcism elevates him as the critical battleground in the war of Good versus Evil, God versus Satan. Who would not be flattered to have such exalted Personages battling over one's soul? The exorcist takes the role of proxy for God; the host plays proxy for Satan. Together they duke it out, though the outcome is certain: Good triumphs over Evil. Ultimately the host's body is exhausted, his worth and value affirmed by God's direct intervention, and the psychodrama is drawn to a close. The host returns to the arms of his weeping family, cleanly absolved of any responsibility for the chaos he orchestrated.

Making Contact

Perhaps the most propitious experience available for direct contact with astral-level entities is using devices allowing them to transmit messages with minimal energy. The widespread use of pendulums, dowsing rods, and Ouija boards testifies to the eternal fascination with communicating with the spirit realm, and the spirit realm's eagerness to participate. In the case of the Ouija board, an astral entity has an opportunity to speak directly, letter by letter, offering a more comprehensive and precisely focused message than a rattling window can offer. There are several cautions to keep in mind, however.

The first caution is to recognize that astral-level entities are just that: souls lodged in the "way station" between physical and spiritual realms. An astral entity possesses little more wisdom than the human being it previously animated. How enlightened is the Average Joe? Send Average Joe to a weekend seminar on spiritual growth and you have an astral entity. What great pearls of wisdom will spring from a disembodied car mechanic? He may be able to offer an "insider's perspective" on the death transition process and his current environs, but that is as far as his spiritual education has progressed.

Average Joe's banal prose aside, there can be a danger in using Ouija boards where the human hosts are too unstable or too trusting. Normally, when a pair sits across a Ouija board and opens themselves up, that openness is expressed vibrationally as a slender tendril rising from the auric fields, breaking the insular "seal" of those fields, making the hosts available to the spirit realm. The tendril provides just enough of a bond that an astral spirit can link with the neurological mechanisms feeding brain impulses to the arm and hand. In an unstable individual, or one desperately hoping for contact with a departed loved one, a larger spout of energy erupts from the auric field, meaning the astral entity can command more of the neurological machinery. This can result in automatic writing, in direct voice transmission, in glossolalia, or in convulsive seizures.

Use of the Ouija board, therefore, can result in opening vibrational channels which, once established and fortified, allow access to entities from levels above the astral. In other words, an astral entity makes the initial contact; once it is evident that the host is capable of sustaining long-term contact and is relatively stable, entities from more advanced levels may link with the host to deliver higher-quality information. The danger of Ouija boards lies with unstable, desperately unhappy individuals searching for help wherever they can find it; their desperation opens larger vibrational channels than is healthy, and their willingness to believe anything they are told may invite an equally unhappy astral entity to abuse their trust by delivering imperious commands or using vulgar language.

A rule of thumb, therefore, in working with Ouija boards or similar devices is to judge the flavor of the material. Is it respectful, genuinely helpful, perceptive, addressed to the issues raised by the pair whose hands rest on the planchette? Or is it nonsensical, vulgar, rambling, pointless drivel? If the former, pursue the project; if the latter, find another source of amusement.

Close Encounters

Most people go through life without ever directly encountering a phantom. Many are occasionally aware of inexplicable presences about them, the occasional dream where it seems a deceased loved one speaks directly, or unusual sounds in the night. But they shrug such incidents off without seriously considering that they have been visited by those from beyond the veil.

What is the best approach to take if one is suddenly aware of a spectral presence and wishes it to depart? Remember that astral entities may participate in earthly events only with the permission of the fleshbound beings they contact. Reacting with fear—which spews an intense, volatile energy—may only further feed an unwelcome visitor. The best approach is two-pronged: attempt to make calm conversation with the presence, then insist that it depart the earth plane and return to its delayed spiritual evolution.

It may be that a spectral presence has a specific piece of information it wishes to impart, or it seeks information about a specific person. Rather than shooing the ghost away on sight, attempt to engage it in "conversation." Speaking calmly and rationally informs the specter that you are aware of its presence even as your lack of fear withholds any vitalizing energy. Tell it that it is the soul of a deceased person and that it does not belong on Earth; what, then, brings it here? Is there something specific it wishes to impart? Finding a way for it to answer a series of yes-or-no questions may elicit the information.

If attempts at communication are unsuccessful, or the being seems to have malevolent intent, cut off dialogue and announce firmly that it is time for the presence to depart, that it does not belong among the living, and that it must continue its spiritual growth by rising above the earth plane. You might repeat a phrase like, "You are no longer a living person, you must leave the earth plane behind, I offer my blessings as you move toward the light." Repeat the phrase until the presence has dissipated.

Our hope is that this essay has illuminated the process through which souls of the departed may make contact with the earth realm; and to reassure that you have nothing to fear from such contact as long as your intentions are pure, your psyche is relatively stable, and your wits are gathered about you. The next time you feel an inexplicable presence, sense a departed loved one close by, or hear the dining room furniture rearranging itself in the dark of night, recognize that all such are manifestations of the interdimensional commerce flowing across the leaky barrier between earthly and spiritual realms. Boo!

7

High Priests on a Leash:
The Spirituality of Cats and Dogs

Anyone who has ever loved a pet cat or dog knows the special qualities of such a relationship: the unambiguous love and devotion the pet offers its master; the easy and uninhibited affection; the steady companionship; and, for some, an almost telepathic link between human and animal, bypassing language in favor of pure thought exchange. Dogs and cats offer a purity and clarity of relationship rarely found among your fellow humans. As with any other aspect of existence this is no accident, no random crossing of evolutionary paths leading to domesticated animals. Rather, the canine and feline families have developed branches intertwined with the human family, interspecies bridges of consciousness which manifest as pet cats and dogs enjoying life among humanity. Let us examine this more closely.

Cats, Dogs, and People: The Primordial Bond

The earth system hosts innumerable species of plant and animal life. Each plant and animal springs from a nonphysical source, a family of consciousness which holds the master template for its expression in the earthly medium. The template holds all probable variations of manifestation, ensuring adaptability to a range of environmental conditions. Some species have a broad, diffuse template allowing its offshoots to range widely over the globe, developing subspecies in diverse ecological niches; other species' offshoots are tightly focused on a specific small area. As a general rule, a family of consciousness will look to enhance its viability and endurance by stretching the boundaries of its form to their utmost potential. Species may appear to "evolve" over time as various probable variations manifest to harmonize with changing environmental conditions.

Feline and canine families of consciousness have developed a unique slant on this process: rather than stretching the boundaries of *form* to ensure their adaptability, these families have forged unique strands of *consciousness* which intertwine with that of humanity. Humanity is a recent arrival on the earth scene, of course, and the feline and canine families thrived for eons before its appearance. But once it was clear that humanity was established, spreading, and likely to become the dominant creature on the planet, the unique potentials of consciousness among feline and canine families were activated.

A number of factors come into play when considering whether a species can form such an intertwined, hybrid consciousness with humanity. First, the animal must be considered attractive by people. It must be the right size: not so small that it is easily and accidentally crushed; not so large that it towers over man and crowds his living space. There must be a mutual sympathy to the overall life purpose of animal and man. And the animal must possess sufficient "rational" intelligence that there can be some meeting of minds across species lines. The number of species meeting all these criteria is fairly small; and only the feline and canine families have developed such potential partnerships to the fullest.

Let us now examine each family of consciousness more closely.

The Feline Family

Of all terrestrial creatures, cats are perhaps the most firmly anchored in "predator-prey" consciousness. If another creature is smaller, they instinctively torment and kill it; if larger, they fear its doing the same to them (though at the "King of the Jungle" level lions have little to fear, smaller cats both seek and become tasty treats). Cats will reflexively flee from the sight of their approaching masters after a lifetime of loving care, so imbued are they with the expectation of attack from creatures larger than they. Cats are built to express predator-prey consciousness to perfection: they can leap many times their height, race at furious speed, climb trees, swim (under protest), sink their claws and fangs into prey, hiss and scratch at attackers. The cat is the sublime expression of "eat or be eaten" consciousness.

It is generally not natural for cats to form relationships outside their family, as every other creature is perceived as either dinner or danger. Still, at the level of families of consciousness, a bond has been bridged with human consciousness as a way of "piggybacking" into areas settled by humanity which might not otherwise support a feline population. This broadens the potential experience available to feline consciousness. In addition, it provides a setting of security, abundance, and consistency, which allows cats to fulfill their deeper mission.

Cats are the explorers and philosophers of the animal world. For the most part they never get the chance to express their deeper nature, for as long as they are caught up in the predator-prey dynamic, they cannot relax their guard long enough to explore and contemplate. Of course we are projecting anthropomorphic qualities onto cats—they are not really philosophers—but there is a sense in which cats serve for the animal world what the Watcher family serves for humanity: that of keen-eyed observers, feeding back to higher realms of consciousness a constant narrative of Earth's un-folding events. On the surface, cats' vigilance serves their predator-prey nature; more deeply, their acute perceptual skills and stealthy patience render them the perfect "eyes and ears" of the animal world.

Because cats are so rooted in the predator-prey dynamic, which demands an immediate appraisal of the nature of every creature it encounters, they are especially keen in observing relationships: in noting how human families and friendships form, grow, and decline. They are upset by angry voices and stomping feet because of their great sensitivity to such issues; they will flee from overwhelming displays of emotion.

Enhancing their observational prowess is the ability to perceive the energy fields surrounding the body; to watch the auric fields flow and flux in response to environmental and human stimuli. This ever-shifting display offers a more truthful picture of others' emotions than words or tone of voice suggest, so it is here that cats place the most stock.

Anyone with a cat knows that cats consider an empty lap a wasted lap, and they will promptly make proper use of it by filling it. Cats seek out close physical contact because they perceive such a richness of information by bathing directly in the energy fields of their human family. Yes, they enjoy the sheer physical warmth as well, but equally important is the whole-body stimulation and depth of information gained by direct perception of human energy fields. As the "observers" of the animal kingdom, they seek out the highest quality of information to pass along to the higher realms, and this they gain while curled up in your lap.

This brings us to another universal quality of cats: their love of napping and sleeping. This isn't laziness, but is rather the compromise solution to a paradox of feline nature: on the one hand they are passive, keen-eyed observers of the world; on the other, they are immersed in the predator-prey dynamic, requiring an alertness that precludes passive observation. As with any creature, sleep is possible only when the ego is certain that danger is at bay and no harm will come while sleeping. Domesticated cats seem to spend an inordinate amount of time in sleep because this is the only way they can suppress their all-consuming predator-prey vigilance and fulfill their role as observers. In sleep, daily experiences are processed and transmitted to the higher realms of consciousness. Cats take "cat naps" throughout the day to send off quick dispatches of unfolding events.

To some extent, the human family of consciousness has come to rely on the feline family's observations as an auxiliary source of information on manifested events. There is a neutrality to cats' observations, while ego-based human consciousness often colors and distorts its transmissions. In some cases, a human family constellation will agree before birth to include one or several feline observers as a way of recording in meticulous neutrality the relationships forged among themselves; to round out their higher selves' perceptions with their pets'. *In a limited sense*, a higher self can project consciousness into a feline offshoot, so that a member of the constellation not choosing human birth may participate as the feline observer. This comes perilously close to suggesting that human souls incarnate as animals, and this is not our intention. A higher self may simply *contribute* to the consciousness of a cat by projecting a strand or two into an already established field of consciousness animating a given cat.

In their wild, natural state, cats are completely immersed in the predator-prey dynamic, and their powers of observation are largely limited to ensuring their safety and hunting prey. Linking with humanity broadens feline consciousness in allowing it to develop its powers of observation to the point where cats make a significant contribution to the Earth's unfolding events by feeding a steady stream of observations to the higher realms of consciousness. They particularly specialize in relationships, both relationships that they develop with people and those they observe among people. They benefit humanity by providing a neutral stream of observation which rounds out human higher selves' perceptions of events.

The Canine Family

As complement to the feline family's passive, observational role, the canine family has developed an active, participatory partnership with humanity.

In their wild state, dogs are also immersed in the predator-prey dynamic, but in both form and consciousness this dynamic is ratcheted down a notch or two. For dogs, hunting and killing prey, and avoiding predators, are important but not all-consuming. Their form is well designed for chasing and killing prey; but they cannot run, leap, climb trees, or seize and immobilize prey with cats' smooth perfection; their form less perfectly reflects the predator-prey dynamic. The canine template has a broader scope, building complex family and tribal relationships; and reveling in earthly life with a lusty exuberance. Cats preen, dogs howl at the moon.

So where feline consciousness is passive and observational, canine consciousness is active and participatory. As with cats, dogs flourished for eons before humanity's appearance, but once this strange, awkwardly designed, two-legged creature began to master its environs, the benefits of linking with humanity became apparent (initially in the form of bones tossed from caves) and the potential link between families of consciousness was activated. Bonding with humanity allowed dogs to deemphasize predator-prey enthrallment, and focus more on the other aspects of their nature—relationships and earth-revel. It also enhanced their participation in the earth system, expanding their numbers and facilitating their geographic spread.

Canine relationships are complex, but the hierarchies are always clear. The dog world is a status culture, where proper deference must be shown to those of higher rank, and groveling and obedience are expected of lower-status members. Dogs have a complex and sophisticated system for determining relative status; you can see this when two dogs meet for the first time and "check each other out"— often in distressingly scatological terms—all the while giving and receiving "rank" signals: from groveling to rolling on their backs to growling to friendly play.

Dogs must always know who the boss is, the alpha male to whom they express obeisance. Because dogs must always have a master, it is natural that they seek out such a master within their human family. They naturally defer to the one who provides the food, for this is one function of the alpha male, to ensure that the pack is properly fed. Once they have chosen their "alpha male," and it may be one or several members of a family, a dog's loyalty, deference, obedience, and even reverence are set for life.

Looking at the human-canine relationship from deeper levels, several issues are involved. One is that the relationship between dog and man is mutually rewarding. As opposed to cats, who often act as if their loving caretakers were an insufferable nuisance, dogs offer tangible benefit to their people. Perhaps of greatest importance is dogs' protective nature, drawing a circle of safety around home and family against the dangers beyond. A dog can easily repel or kill intruders, even human intruders, with a swiftness and deadly certainty no unarmed human can match. It is canine nature to defend the pack, and this trait easily carries into relationships with people. There is a measure of self-interest as well, of course, for a dog protecting its master is protecting its own supply of food and care.

Dogs offer a simplicity of emotion; a purity of love, devotion, and adoration. No human relationship, except that between parent and infant, offers such unadulterated purity; for as soon as a child is old enough to express his independent will, that will begins clashing with the world, and that clash continues to the last breath. As part of the original canine-human partnership, therefore, it was understood that dogs would provide the distilled purity of love and loyalty as a buffer against the bruising emotional discord that often clouds human life. Dogs provide a refuge, a safe haven where one is always welcome, valued, and loved just for being oneself. Small children especially benefit from canine companionship, for their simple, pure emotions blend well with canine nature. And men, whose emotional lives are often stunted in your culture, may look to dogs as their truest friends, finding in their four-legged companions a loyalty and unambiguous love they cannot find among their own.

Thus, dogs offer an emotional buffer to human life, feeding into the human circle a purity of love and devotion that balances the bruising complexities of human relationships. The intent is to provide an external source of warmth and love independent of other people, ensuring that no one need be completely bereft of loving companionship as long as a dog is within reach. Dogs are no substitute for the richness of human relationships, of course, but they offer a cushion of emotional security against life's vicissitudes. Especially in a time of social and familial upheaval, dogs' emotional buffer helps keep people more stable and grounded than they would otherwise be.

Again, without suggesting that human souls reincarnate as animals, there are situations where a higher self projects a strand or two of consciousness into a canine offshoot as a way either of experiencing emotion from a dog's pure simplicity, or serving as a companion to a particular individual. Higher selves specializing in the emotional domain often seek to experience emotion from all possible angles, and the dog's emotional clarity, and ability to participate tangentially in complex human relations, helps to "round out" a higher self's store of emotional experience. At the same time, if a higher self desires to participate with another soul in an earthly experience without manifesting in human form, projecting strands of intent into canine form may provide enough of a connection that the relationship reaches satisfactory fulfillment.

The Spiritual Life of Dogs and Cats

In *Earthly Cycles* we described the many qualities of the soul that the higher self manipulates in creating the personality template of a given offshoot, one human life. Among these qualities are family of consciousness, soul age, soul aspect, life theme, and more. To what extent are the animal families of consciousness governed by similar matrices? What are the differences?

Several points should be immediately apparent. One is that there is greater variability in human personality than among the animal families. Animals may be high-strung or relaxed, friendly or reserved, trusting or suspicious, but they generally do not reach the extremes of autism, genius, schizophrenia, or suicide that mark the far reaches of the human psyche. In animals the psyche is constructed with a large core of species uniformity, atop which are sprinkled unique variabilities; in humanity the core of uniformity is relatively small, while the area for variability is commensurately larger.

In part this reflects the greater complexity of the human psyche—a rational mind, afire with art and spirit, anchored to a mal-adapted body in a challenging environment—and in part it reflects humanity's greater emphasis on emotional life. Whatever the fruits of man's technological prowess or intellectual mastery, in the end it is the content of one's *emotional* life that determines the ultimate meaning of a lifetime, for relationships are where you live, suffer, triumph, and grow. In dogs and cats, as we have seen, the deeper purpose for participating in earthly life lies elsewhere: in the preda-tor-prey dynamic, in raw physicality, in hierarchies of relationship. So the many soul qualities manipulated by a human higher self are not available in such richness to the canine and feline families of consciousness. Thus, there is a greater homogeneity of personality among those families than among their human companions.

Where variability is expressed in the canine family, it is through the different breeds. Here the differences are in *form* and *function* rather than emotional variability. Whether dogs fetch downed geese, herd sheep, detect cocaine, or guard their family, form is matched to function. Size, shape of ears and noses, and so on, are varied to pre-cisely reflect the aptitudes of a particular breed. Each breed, develop-ing as a subspecies of the canine family, develops a distinct personality template as well. Some breeds are noted for their gentle-ness and ease with children; others are high-strung and vicious toward strangers. When humanity develops dog breeds through controlled breeding, it controls the *form*, which in turn calls down certain personality strands matched to that form. Thus, humanity can control the soul qualities of its canine companions by manipulating the form those pets can take. This mirrors the division of human con-sciousness into seven families of consciousness, but without the sharp divisions of working and intellectual life marking those families.

There is less variability among cats. Because dogs are active participants in earthly and human life, their variety in form ensures adaptability to a wide range of environmental and working condi-tions. Cats, the cool observers, need only one bodily template that works well in a variety of climatic conditions. Because they do not participate in human activities, they do not require the canines' broad variability of form.

There is a progression of "soul age" among companion animals, but less so than for humanity. Again, the boundaries of variability are more tightly drawn. A "baby soul" dog might focus on raw physicality: the hunt, mating, protection of pack are the all-consuming focuses; among domesticated dogs, the more savage breeds, and those loving the master and distrusting all others, are the "baby souls" of the breed. "Young soul" dogs are more playful, easier of temperament, more generally welcoming of other animals and people. "Mature soul" dogs are often the alpha male or his mate, for their greater wisdom and cunning, and ability to command and control the complex relationships within the pack, serve the pack well. Among domesticated dogs, mature souls tend to shy away from raw work, instead putting their energies into "supervising" the lives of their masters' families by looking after small children, fetching the paper, and so on. And "old soul" dogs can hardly bring themselves to lift a paw unless genuine danger threatens them or their families; they expect to be treated as equal members of the family and will not stoop to cheap circus tricks like fetching sticks or rolling over.

Interestingly, the continuum from baby souls to old souls is reflected in form: baby- and young-soul dogs tend to be smaller in size; mature- and old-soul dogs are larger. This arises, in part, because smaller animals have to focus more energy on establishing and maintaining their territories and rights while larger animals take their security more for granted and can relax their guard.

Of the two species, cats are more "spiritual" than dogs because their role as cool observers of earth and human activities carries with it a direct connection to the higher realms to which they feed their flow of observation. In this sense, all cats are "old souls" because they directly and deeply sense the larger bodies of consciousness from which they spring. They observe, they sleep, they keep themselves clean and above the fray.

Do animal souls reincarnate? In *Earthly Cycles* we proposed a model of reincarnation which abandoned the traditional notion of a single soul recycling itself into a succession of bodies; rather, the higher self projects offshoots, single souls, into a number of simultaneously occurring lifetimes. The soul of an individual does not "come back" time and again, but is reabsorbed into the higher self, with any unresolved karma projected into other offshoots. The higher self cannot release earthly experience until all karma created by its offshoots is dissolved.

Perhaps you can see how the soul life of animals differs from the human reincarnational process. What compels humans to return in body after body is karma—and karma is created only when the intent to cause harm is married to action causing harm. Are animals capable of such deliberate infliction of cruelty on others? They are designed to kill, yes, but only for sustenance or to protect themselves or their pack. They lack the complex emotional and rational qualities that allow humans to murder over money, jealousy, or revenge. They do not kill for sport—even the cat's taunting and batting of a mouse is free of the willful intention to inflict suffering. Because animals' psychological nature is more elementary and instinctually rooted, the key element of "intent to cause harm" is largely absent. Thus, dogs and cats do not weave karmic braids compelling reincarnational resolution.

As a rule, the souls of individual cats and dogs are reabsorbed into their higher selves with no need for returning to the earth plane to resolve unfinished business. At times, however, given the number of cat or dog lifetimes that can play out across the span of a human life, a pet enjoying a powerful relationship with its master can, upon death, project certain strands of intent into a successor offshoot. This provides a base of continuity, an easy familiarity, with which a kitten or puppy works its way into the heart of its new owner; a person may feel a tinge of recognition when meeting the eyes of such a new pet. It is not accurate to say the old pet has reincarnated into the new, but that certain strands of consciousness have carried over into the new form, providing a foundation of familiarity between pet and master.

Pet Hints

Given the material we have outlined thus far, we can close with a few suggestions on how to enhance your relationship with your pet dog or cat to ensure that its soul purpose is being fulfilled.

For cats: Recognizing that cats are here to observe your life and environs with cool detachment, first ensure that your cat feels safe. To fulfill their mission, cats must feel sufficiently secure that they can relax their predator-prey consciousness and bring calm "observation" to the forefront of attention. A physically abused cat is miserable, for it depends on its abusive master for sustenance and shelter while the abuse renders it incapable of relaxing into observational calm.

Next, to the extent possible, allow cats to be in close physical contact with you. The direct immersion in your energy fields offers them the highest quality of information, which they in turn transmit to the higher realms. Allow as much lap sitting and shared sleeping as you can stand.

Finally, talk with your cat. Tell it in rich detail and extravagant emotional gestures what is happening in your life. Notice how a cat will hold its attention on such soliloquies long after a fellow human would have fled or fallen asleep. The words may not be understood but the emotional content is, and serves to enrich the cat's picture of what happens in your life beyond the confines of your shared space.

For dogs: Dogs are here to revel in earthy physicality and to serve you as faithful companions. The best way to fulfill these needs is to have them accompany you in physical activity: taking walks together, going shopping, swimming, hiking, working in the garden. If they cannot directly contribute to the work at hand, at least do not exclude them for getting in the way; they are miserable if they feel they have violated their covenant of service. Find ways for your dog to be useful, or engage it in mutually rewarding play, to allow it fulfillment of its dog essence.

Because dogs are physically oriented, they don't require much in the way of monologues. They resonate more with action. For them, love is action, loyalty is action, friendship is action. Find active ways of having them fulfill their desire to serve and they will reward you with selfless love and devotion.

Finally, in that you have incarnated in the earth system to experience as broad a wealth of experience as possible, including dogs and cats in your life and home whenever possible can only enhance your life's store of experience. They both surprise and delight you with their own personalities and behavior; and trigger protective "alpha" behaviors in you. Your life will be immeasurably richer for sharing the journey with a four-pawed friend.

8

Into the Dreamtime:
The Soul's Nightly Journey

Every culture, from aboriginal tribe to complex civilization, recognizes the significance and esoteric mystery of dreams. History, literature, and poetry swarm with dreams' prophetic and symbolic power. Modern western thought, its vision narrowed by the blinders of materialism, struggles to make sense of dreams. In one view, the purpose of sleep is to allow the body time to rest and heal, with dreaming a mysterious byproduct. Dreams are variously explained as the random static of neurological chaos; a means of emotionally processing the day's events; or the symbolic patina on material rising from the deeper strata of the psyche. Whatever one's view, all agree that the realm of sleep and dreaming remains a dark mystery.

We begin our journey through the realm of sleep with a broad overview of its meaning and purpose, then tread step by step through the stages and levels of the dreamtime world. To begin, we explore the nature of earthbound, animate life.

The Wall of Illusion

You live in a "camouflage" physical system, meaning the swarming ocean of energy and vibration in which you live is never perceived directly. Creatures inhabiting such a system limit their perception to the few slender bands of vibration their senses perceive. Even these few fragmentary strands are not perceived "as they are," but are filtered and interpreted by the brain to construct a cohesive picture of sight, sound, and tactile sensation. The result is that each species weaves its own fragmentary, hallucinatory picture of "reality" from the swirling clouds of vibration which envelop the earth.

The purpose of such a system is to emphasize the supremacy of the *individual*, by rendering invisible the cosmic web in which you are embedded; convincing you that "you" end neatly at the skin, separate and distinct from other creatures and the natural world. Not only do you not perceive the cosmic soup in which you swim; but your senses are tuned to block perception of the energy fields swirling around every living thing, plant or animal. Your senses tell you that you stand alone, distinct and separate; while in reality you are embedded in a swarming ocean of energy.

While your conscious mind clings to its waking perceptions as "real" and struggles to make sense of its dreamtime imagery, the fact is that you must sleep and dream because maintaining the illusions of physical life places great strain on consciousness, which must be "relieved" by restoration to its natural state. In other words, the realm of sleep and dreams is the native state of consciousness, and operates according to natural principles, whereas the illusion of physical reality is a self-generated hallucination which can be sustained for only so long before consciousness must seek relief from operating in such an unnatural state.

While you naturally focus on the externalities of life—your family and friends, career, money, health—there is a far deeper purpose to your being. This purpose was determined by your higher self before incarnation, was sculpted into your personality template at the time of birth, and remains the overarching blueprint of your existence. Chances are you do not know what it is; for it remains veiled from conscious awareness even as it informs every moment of your life.

At night, when you release the illusion of physical life and return to your natural state, you commune with your higher self to compare your experiences to the life theme and goals it has established. Progress and backsliding are noted; probable events are vitalized which will steer you toward relevant experience; and you draw upon the wisdom and experience of probable and reincarnational selves playing out their lives in private cocoons of history. All this occurs while also relieving the strain of the waking self's daily journey through the unnatural realm of physical experience.

The Wall of the Self

Two "selves" are involved in the dream exchange: the authentic self and the waking self. The authentic self is the "real" you, a body of consciousness composed of your higher self, your reincarnational and probable selves, and the unique soul or individualized spark of consciousness that animates your mind and body. Probable and reincarnational selves, along with the soul, are embedded within the higher self, which in turn is cocooned within even greater bodies of consciousness. This is the real you, the authentic self.

The ego is one element of the waking self. The ego is tightly focused on me-me-me, on fulfillment of rudimentary needs for food, shelter, clothing, etc. Once those needs are met—or even if they're not—higher levels of waking consciousness complement the ego's feral focus; just as the brain holds varying levels of complexity from primitive brain stem to evolved cerebrum. Familial ties, friendship, the fruits of art and intellect and spirit—all these flow from the more expansive waking self.

For you to function at all effectively in the world of physical illusion, there must be a wall of separation between waking and authentic selves. You could not safely navigate through physical reality while your consciousness was bombarded with cosmic energies; your brain would collapse under the strain. The wall of separation is nothing more than a difference in the frequencies on which the two realms operate. The ego, holding the body's safety as its primary concern, tightens its focus to the slow, dense frequencies perceived by the senses; while the faster frequencies of natural consciousness whir undetected. The wall is not so much a wall as a gap, a chasm between levels of frequency.

Three factors contribute to how permeable or rigid the boundary between waking and authentic selves will be: earth vibration, cultural cosmology, and personality. The earth rides crests and troughs of accelerating and decelerating frequency, bobbing through immense oceans of time as its core vibration quickens and slows. In an age of slower earth vibrations, the frequency gap widens, pushing waking and authentic selves farther apart. Life coarsens as inspiration and vision dry up. When the earth's core vibration accelerates, the frequency gap narrows; with a narrower chasm to cross, waking and authentic selves communicate more robustly: life is buoyed by artistic and spiritual inspiration.

A culture's cosmology, its fundamental beliefs and values, also influences the permeability between dimensions. Cultures rooted in communion with nature and spirit, who hear their ancestors whisper on the wind, recognize the sacredness of earth and its creatures, and seek visions and inspirational dreams, naturally enjoy easy communion between waking and authentic selves. Cultures strongly focused on material experience, carrying a sharp rational focus and a disdain for mystical insight, naturally close themselves off from easy communion with their authentic selves.

Finally, an individual's personal psychology influences the boundary's permeability. Each higher self carries its own vibration and intent, which in turn flow from a higher family of consciousness carrying a unique vibrational matrix. Each incarnation is established with a personality template sculpted into its auric fields, to tether experience to life theme. Layered atop this congenital constitution will be childhood experiences either embracing or ignoring the fruits of the authentic self: precognitive dreams, the presence of invisible "friends," past-life recall, extrasensory perception. Taken together, the earth's vibration, a culture's cosmology, and an individual's personality and childhood experience blend to determine the relative permeability of the boundary between waking and authentic selves.

Breaching the Wall

Before you can fall asleep, you must feel safe and secure; for the ego must be convinced to release its protective vigilance over your body's safety. Indeed, you deliberately seek out a sanctuary offering little stimulation—a dark, quiet room, neither too cold nor too hot—as the ideal setting in which your ego can be convinced to relax its guard. You lie down, laying your head upon or closer to the earth than during waking hours, surrendering to its deep, elemental pull.

The ego evaporates as you fall asleep. With no need to maintain sharp concern for your body's safety, and with your consciousness flowing across the boundary toward its authentic self, the ego disintegrates. It doesn't go anywhere; it decays into oblivion. Each morning, upon awaking, you reconstruct yourself, gathering together your store of memory, desire, and emotion, stitching them together into a cohesive personality which others instantly recognize from the day before. Each day you reinvent yourself anew.

With the ego's low, earth-based frequency dissolving, consciousness is liberated to flow toward its natural frequencies. The early, light stages of sleep are a period of gradual acceleration of consciousness; the day's experiences are processed during this transitional phase, teased apart into their physical/emotional/mental/spiritual components, examined for their relevance or irrelevance to one's life theme, evaluated for their significance to life's deeper purpose. In a sense, this is a period of sifting and sorting through the mementos and souvenirs of each day's earthly experience, separating the precious from the petty.

The petty are immediately "discarded," in the sense that they are dismissed from further processing. Those experiences ripe with significance are retained and passed on to higher levels of consciousness for more meticulous examination. This early, light phase of sleep still operates through the boundary between waking and authentic selves, and ensures that only deeply significant events pass through to higher levels of consciousness.

As sleep deepens, the boundary dissolves, as the ego has dissolved, and consciousness is free to soar to its natural frequencies. A slender strand of vibration remains anchored to the body, feeding its perceptions directly to the higher realms of consciousness rather than the (now nonexistent) ego. This strand must be maintained, not only to ensure the body's continued security, but to sustain the flow of vitalizing energy from the higher self, without which bodily death ensues. (This strand of vibration is often referred to as a "silver cord" in astral travel accounts.)

Deep Communion

The phase of deep communion can be envisioned as multiple strands of consciousness, humming at varying frequencies, intermingling and exchanging tendrils of information across permeable boundaries. The energies involved do not meld into a homogenous soup of undifferentiated consciousness, but retain individual identity even as they strive to harmonize their vibrations to foster deepest communion. The waking self's consciousness must "ascend"—accelerating its vibration—while the higher self "descends"—

decelerating its furious whirl—and they meet on common ground, at a mutually compatible frequency. Other contributors, probable and reincarnational selves, do not slow their vibrations as much as they must purify their vibrational tones, shaking off the distinct accents of their private worlds.

Since all time is simultaneous, all probable and reincarnational selves live out their lives in the same "place" and "time." What distinguishes one from another is the unique vibrational tone of each probable earth, which locks every participating entity into perceiving only activity occurring within that narrow slice of reality. Linear time is a track of gradually accelerating pulsations; here again, a participating entity chooses to be born at a specific moment-pulsation and rides the gentle acceleration over a lifetime's span; any event lying outside that stretch of pulsation will be lost to the senses. In very simple terms, this is how probable and reincarnational selves live out their lives in other "times" and "places" even as the higher self perceives them as one simultaneous whirl.

In the dream state, these unique vibrational accents are sloughed off, like actors shedding costumes after a performance, the better to meet one another in a state of pure consciousness. No strand of consciousness married to form can ever completely release the residue of its earth-based form, and there is something of a United Nations atmosphere to communion among probable and reincarnational selves, each bearing the unique accent of its home reality.

Many factors affect the degree to which a given self can shed its earth-based identity and participate in deep communion. A physical body's overall vibration falls somewhere on a scale between "dense" and "ethereal" based on its weight (overweight being a dense vibration); its health (illness or chronic pain tilts the scale toward "dense"); whether one ate a rich meal shortly before retiring; whether one impairs the body's harmony through injurious diet, drink, or smoking; whether one is consumed with anxiety over the morrow's anticipations; whether one tends toward spirit or vice. An overweight smoker worried about losing his job is less able to shed his earth-based energies and participate fully in deep communion than a vegetarian yogi meditating in stress-free reverie.

So probable and reincarnational selves bring lesser and greater degrees of openness and purity to their exchange during deep communion. The higher self, floating above earth-based activity, carries no residue from its realm and offers its pure, unblemished energy to each offshoot strand. It is each offshoot's condition that determines its clarity of communion with its higher self.

Here is where this seemingly esoteric discussion meets real-world, practical application: your waking experience is profoundly influenced by the nocturnal process of deep communion, yet the purity and fidelity of that exchange is affected by the condition of your body and thoughts. Further, the waking self's ability to translate insights gleaned from deep communion into practical benefit is influenced by the condition of body and mind.

In deep communion, the individual strands of consciousness rising from probable and reincarnational selves intertwine with strands flowing from the higher self, and at the point of intersection a rich vibrational dialogue ensues. Powerful daytime events, the body's overall health, the swelling tide of thought—all these are carried as vibrational matrices flowing from each individualized soul to its higher self. The higher self evaluates these strands in light of its intended growth and experience for a lifetime, to determine whether the waking self is "on track" or veering off into unanticipated, and possibly detrimental, paths of experience.

Freedom and free will are the cornerstones of the camouflage system, and a higher self never directly intervenes in the lives of its offshoots. It sets them up with certain characteristics, tethers them to a specific life theme, selects a birth mother, and then releases them. From there, the waking self takes over, aided by the powerful but undetected influence of the higher self. Final choices always rest with the waking self; it has every power and right to backslide into retrograde and primitive behaviors despite its higher self's expectation of growth toward enlightenment.

At the nexus between each offshoot and its higher self during deep communion, after the offshoot has offered vibratory fragments of its day's experience, the higher self offers a flow of responsive material. Couched in dispassionate respect, the higher self proffers its comparison of the offshoot's anticipated growth versus its actual experience. The great probable swirl of potential choices is laid before the offshoot, the better for it to understand how it came to actualize one slender strand and what alternative potentials lie ahead. The danger of further entwining karmic ties with others, as opposed to loosening them, is emphasized, for all karmic bonds must be dissolved before earthly life can be released.

Each offshoot also shares, to a greater or lesser degree, information and experience with its brethren offshoots. Where several offshoots are set up with similar life challenges, a rich dialogue sharing their experiences across the centuries enriches and revitalizes those involved. If two heads are better than one, a dozen probable selves are even better! In other cases, life situations may be so starkly disparate that only an occasional "greeting" is shared. The insight and inspiration you may occasionally feel upon awaking—a sudden zest to face your challenges with redoubled vigor and determination—stems from deep communion with your brethren selves offering their wisdom for your benefit.

To sum up: in deep communion each offshoot offers its day's experiences to the higher self, which responds with a flow of guidance and direction to encourage the offshoot to stay the steady course of growth toward enlightenment and release of karmic bonds. Among probable and reincarnational selves, experiences and wisdom are swapped in a free-flowing exchange which encourages all participants to face their waking challenges with renewed strength and creativity.

Into the Dreamtime

Why do dreams so often seem chaotic and confusing? They seem so because what transpires during the dream state and what is recalled upon awaking are two sharply distinct processes. Recalled dreams represent your conscious mind's best effort to make sense of material of a frequency and depth which it is not designed to process. Raw dream material must be decelerated many levels of frequency to be processed by the conscious mind, losing fidelity and richness in the process. The seemingly random chaos of dream imagery stems from the brain's inability to coherently synthesize the raw stuff of dreams, which operates on a different, deeper logic and order.

If you showed a film by Bergman or Fellini to a small child and asked what he saw, he would deliver a crude plot synopsis stripped of all symbolism, philosophy, and iconography. So it is with the waking mind's interpretation of dreams.

Waking consciousness organizes itself according to linear principles, especially linear time. When you recall an experience you replay it in from start to finish; when you tell your life story you begin with childhood and retrace your steps forward. Because linear time is a parameter only of matter-based systems, it plays no part in the greater dimensions where the higher self resides and whence dream material arises. As a result, when waking consciousness forces nonlinear experience into a linear-time sequence, not only will coherence be lost, but the *significance* will be lost as well.

The signposts by which the higher self evaluates your life journey are not linear, factual, logical, or rational. They are *emotional*. That is, the material rising from waking self to higher self does not reflect the everyday mechanics and worries of your life—wealth, health, career—but carries the *emotional impact* of your life experience. While your conscious mind navigates the material world through reason and logic, it is your *heart* that records the true measure of your experience. Whatever your life theme and tasks may be, it is your emotional life that generates the most significant milestones of triumph or calamity on the rocky road to fulfillment.

Thus, the higher self evaluates the emotional content of each day's events as its primary source material; the physical wrapping on those events is discarded. Did you feel love, jealousy, fear, enmity, anger, guilt, triumph, or pain? Did you feel nothing at all? Is your emotional life a healthy, rollicking flow of freely expressed feelings, or a bottleneck of choked repression? These are the vital indicators of your life's progress.

With that as background, we can briefly explore several sources of dream material. The first is what might be called Probable Drama School, whose source material is the ego's choices pulling certain probable futures toward manifestation. In the dream state, these probabilities can be projected, as onto a movie screen, and played out, the better to evaluate their potential results. While a soul can perform this on its own, there is a certain joy and camaraderie in joining with other reincarnational and probable selves to create a mutual drama, richer for the greater insights of all involved.

Generally, at least several and as many as a dozen different scenarios will be played out, depending on the apparent strength of crystallizing probabilities. While this process may appear fanciful and inconsequential to your waking experience, in truth *your life is profoundly guided by dreamtime dramas enacted by your soul and authentic self.* In the case of almost every significant life event, your authentic self *has already played it out and knows the outcome* and your later physical experience is but a "confirmation version" of what has already transpired.

This is no way limits your freedom to make life choices, or denigrates the importance of physical experience, but it underscores the profound effect your authentic self has on waking experience. For the probable scenarios played out in dreamtime are fed to your waking self—crunched down into remembered dreams—and serve as warnings or blessings on the life choices you contemplate. This enhances your freedom and ability to make wise choices as you already carry, in subliminal awareness, the likely outcomes of choices you ponder. Perhaps you can recall such dreams, where you awoke with a powerful emotional resonance and imagery of a future event hovering in the future.

We have focused on the individual soul's use of probability projection, but of course you do not travel life's journey alone; and it is only through joining with others that you generate the emotional experiences central to your life theme. Where two or more are joined in a relationship that carries its own bundle of probable futures, these too will be sorted out and projected in the dream state as mutually created dramas. Each soul can then evaluate its likely experience and feed counsel to its waking self.

On a broader scale, each culture and era plays hosts to certain themes and concepts, and all souls living at a given time are bonded in a communal enterprise, with each waking self allotted a tiny portion. Mass events are organized and projected, and roles chosen, during communal dreamtime councils. This holds for all mass events, from a two-vehicle car crash to world war. All choose to participate, all choose the scenario to manifest, all choose their roles. Inquisitor and heretic, martyr and priest, king and peasant, prisoner and liberator—all participate in dreamtime dramas, choose their roles, and feed their choices to their waking selves.

The Higher Self Report Card

Another major source of dream material is the higher self's evaluation of each day's emotional mementos, judged against a lifetime's theme, tasks, and karma. The higher self liberates its soul fragment at birth and cannot intervene to force it to fulfill its tasks, or even to prevent the waking self from digging itself into deeper karmic ruts. The ego, a curiously obtuse and maddeningly blind creature from the higher self's perspective, holds ultimate authority over the waking self's experience. The higher self can only evaluate each day's events for evidence that the life purpose is being at least partially fulfilled.

The challenge from the waking self's perspective is that life themes are impressed into the personality at a given "default" intensity which requires concerted effort to transcend. A life theme of poverty-wealth, for instance, may be strongly skewed toward the "poverty" pole, meaning that scarcity and lack come far more naturally than abundance. A theme of intimacy-isolation, if weighted toward isolation, naturally results in an adulthood of comfortable but not intimate friendships and avoidance of romantic intimacy.

From the ego's perspective, it is more comfortable to remain at its default point, even of poverty or isolation, than to do the hard and bruising work of overcoming that default and sliding along the continuum toward greater happiness. Since the ego naturally seeks pleasure and avoids pain, it shuns the bruising trauma stirred up by struggling to override its thematic default; thus, the ego serves as a hindrance to its own happiness! One cannot ascribe human emotion to higher selves, but there is something akin to bewilderment and exasperation at the ego's bull-headed insistence on remaining in a familiar misery rather than struggling toward higher fulfillment—not unlike the sorrow parents feel when their children fall short of their potential and settle for a lesser life.

One tool the higher self has at its disposal is the nightly dreamtime communion with its offshoot soul (blessedly stripped of its guardian ego!). Here, in Probable Drama School, are enacted in rich intensity those grand triumphs awaiting the waking self if it would but make the effort. These enticing potentials are fed from the higher self to the waking self and are the source of the constant "if only" chatter in your interior monologue—if only I had more money, more time, more love, more children; if only I were more spiritual, more creative, more healthy, more successful, *then I would be happy.* The constant yearning for something more, something better, as the key to happiness is the ego's crude way of making sense of whispers from the higher self that your life's highest potential is not yet fulfilled.

Hands Across Time

A third significant source of dream material is the communion among reincarnational selves. Because all incarnations flow from a single higher self, with its narrowly focused soul qualities, all incarnations are bound, like blood brothers, to a common unity of purpose. However diverse the lifetime scenarios crafted by the higher self, they all share a deep thematic commonality. Reincarnational offshoots are thus of great value to each other as they exchange experience and wisdom across the millennia.

Because they all share an overriding goal—overcoming their challenges and realizing fulfillment—and because they are bound to a common thematic focus, reincarnational selves share what seems to "work" and what does not in their respective corners of history. Working with the gradual acceleration of earth's frequency, which carries humanity toward a higher spiritual wisdom, reincarnational selves can "plot" which choices and behaviors would be most effective in a given age.

For example, if a higher self were focused on the theme of slavery-freedom, especially the struggle to overthrow slavery, it would plant incarnational seeds along the linear time continuum to see how those objecting to slavery fared through the millennia. A slave in ancient Egypt or seventeenth-century America who bitterly and publicly denounced the institution that enslaved him would quickly find himself relieved of the burdens of his captive flesh. The nineteenth century was the richest field of action, with abolitionists finally drawing even with, then surpassing, the forces of inertia, tradition, and racism. A historian railing against the evils of slavery in the twenty-fifth century would draw uncomprehending stares: "Slavery? What was that?"

By plotting the cultural reactions and personal experiences of the slavery-freedom theme in its evolution through time, incarnational selves can determine which cultures and eras best play host to that theme. In ancient Egypt the protest was futile; in the nineteenth century it was the age's fundamental crisis; in the distant future it will be irrelevant. To fully engage the theme, to steep everyday life in its bitter essence, one must live in an era making the transition between unthinking acceptance of slavery and its abolition. By pooling their experiences, incarnational selves round out the higher self's store of slavery-freedom experience, and offer suggestions and encouragement to each other as they play out their tiny roles in the broader drama.

Back to the Present

The ideal range for an adult nighttime of sleep is between five and eight hours. Any less and the waking self is cheated of adequate communion time with its authentic self; any more and the body's vitality flags for its overlong immobility. Any artificial interruption of the waking process—whether from alarm clock or screaming child—sabotages the phase most useful to the waking self.

The process of waking up ideally takes at least an hour as dreamtime frequencies gradually decelerate toward the slower, denser vibrations of matter; and the focus shifts from authentic to waking self. While no active dreaming occurs at this stage, it is nonetheless highly critical, for this is when the information, advice, and encouragement gathered during dreamtime are gently fed to the waking self. These gentle waves of wisdom wash across the boundary between authentic and waking selves, even as that boundary is fortified by the inchoate ego. The hope is that some tendrils of wisdom will be retained in awareness, acknowledged and acted upon by the ego as it seeks, however clumsily, to steer you toward fulfillment.

The ego is constructed "from scratch" each morning. The higher self follows a standard template of psychological and physiological maturation which carries the body from infancy to old age, and shapes waking consciousness with qualities appropriate for its body's age. Each day brings body and mind one small 24-hour step forward on its journey, and minute adjustments will be made to reflect that growth.

Atop the standard maturational template, the higher self carries the fruits of each night's deep communion, which it impresses into waking awareness. Finally, the fragments of memory, identity, and purpose—the "who am I?"—left over from the previous day are restored to waking consciousness. This is the ego's structure—a foundational maturational template, the fruits of deep communion, and memory-identity fragments retained by the higher self. Stitched together upon awaking, this makes you *you.*

Here is where the greatest barrier lies to receiving guidance from the higher self. The ego, a cacophonous scrum of fears, neuroses, ambitions, vices, needs, and moral quandaries, has its hands full attending to immediately present experience, and has little time or incentive to shift into a contemplative mood and commune with its higher self. Suffering under the illusion of separation, which triggers constant fear for the body's security and a sense of want, the ego tends to operate from a primitive, survivalist mode. This is not always the case, of course: when you are relaxed, well fed, in the company of loved ones, your ego loosens to embrace the fruits of art and culture and relationship. Nonetheless, the higher self must struggle to impress its daily gleanings upon the waking self against an onslaught of sensory impressions and wants/needs/fears consuming the ego.

The same factors that inhibit the soul's full participation in deep communion tend to hinder communication between higher and waking selves as well. A diseased or neglected body, a mind clouded with worry and struggle, a hostile or dangerous living environment, all contribute to the ego's furious chatter drowning out subtle messages from the higher self.

The irony is that those most in need of clear, direct guidance from the higher self are the least likely to hear its gentle counsel, or risk implementing its suggestions for an altered life course. Perhaps you have known individuals who seem trapped in a downward spiral of multiplying crises—physical, emotional, and personal—where each calamity seems to trigger still another disaster. Most often such snowballing crises are triggered because the ego simply will not stop to consider the soundness of its actions; the higher self can only watch as the ego tumbles into despair, the body into illness, and personal relations into heartbreak. Only when they hit rock-bottom do such people become receptive to guidance from the higher self.

Another factor influencing the ego's embrace of its higher self's guidance is cultural conditioning. Where a culture is steeped in a mystical atmosphere of dreams, visions, and a world swarming with spirit, the barrier between waking and higher selves is elastic and permeable. Where rationalism holds sway, and dreams and visions are regarded as hallucinatory fragments, the barrier is rigid and impenetrable. This cultural norm sets the standard for interdimensional communication, atop which each individual either tightens or loosens the barrier.

Opening to Your Higher Self

We have seen that every night, in the dream state, your soul communes with your higher self and probable/reincarnational brethren, and carries guidance and advice back from its nocturnal sojourn. Given the choice, most people would readily say they welcome such guidance, yet they struggle to hear but the faintest echoes flowing from the higher realms. What tools are available to loosen the barrier between waking self and higher self?

First, one must recognize a cold truth: the higher self's plan for a lifetime may horrify the ego. The ego's wants are simple: shelter, food, love, sex, health, money: as much and as often as possible. There is nothing wrong with desiring any of these; they all contribute to a stable, comfortable life. But here lies the challenge to even the most evolved ego: the higher self may consider fulfillment of these wants an *impediment* to its life plan.

A higher self may determine that, to balance lives of regal opulence, an offshoot should experience a lifetime of poverty. Or suffer victimhood to balance lives of oppressive abuse of power. An offshoot of the Agitator family of consciousness is virtually compelled to live outside the mainstream as an object of scorn and derision, with violent death at the hands of the authorities or outraged villagers considered (by the higher self) a triumphant finale. A lifetime of chronic ill health offers a rich immersion into the body and its complex workings and failings.

Do you still want to know your higher self's plan for your life?

The point is not that you surrender to fatalistic endurance of the life sculpted by your monstrous higher self, but that you recognize that the ego's wants—Perfect Love, Perfect Health, Perfect Wealth—are irrelevant to your life's deeper purpose. Since the ego always has the "upper hand" in communion with the higher self, it can concoct infinite diversions to block hearing its subtle messages. To truly breach the barrier, one must convince the ego to relax and open to wisdom flowing from the higher realms.

Deep Communion Journal

One of the most effective ways of doing this is to use the hazy bookends of sleep, as you fall asleep and then awake the next morning. Since the ego dissolves as you surrender to sleep, using this time as a conscious conduit to the higher realms is more effective than during the waking hours. You might speak aloud phrases carrying your desires in clear, simple prose: "I open myself to whatever guidance my higher self has to offer"; "I seek guidance on (a particular problem)"; "I wish to consciously know and fulfill my life's purpose." You would not use this time to ask the higher self to fulfill an ego-based need for money, love, or health. You are not telling the higher self to manufacture your life to the ego's specifications, but to open yourself to whatever the higher self wishes to impart.

At the other end of sleep, upon awaking in the morning, again you can take advantage of the ego's inchoate, fragmented state to absorb the guidance gleaned from the night's deep communion. Keeping a journal at your bedside is an excellent tool for training yourself to consciously recall the fruits of deep communion. It is important not to *judge* the material as it flows—for this is allowing the ego to jump into the process—but to simply record whatever impressions and fragments arise. There may be recalled dream material, or diffuse feelings and thoughts not bound to dream imagery. Do not compare this material with the desires stated at the cusp of sleep the prior evening; just record it.

Over time, this process of verbally requesting information, and recording the results the next morning, fosters a rich interdimensional communion. Consistency is important, for that communion deepens with each night's exchange. Patterns should emerge in the recorded entries, consistent themes and symbols which reveal the higher self's intended purpose for your life, and whether you are "on track" or "off track." Bursts of sudden inspiration or urges to make major life shifts may well result from a consistently followed program.

Waking Dreams

Another powerful tool culled from deep communion is "waking dreams." You are familiar with the process of dream interpretation, where fragments of dream imagery are stripped of their symbolic clothing and analyzed. Here the process is reversed. Taking a situation which arises in your waking life, you reduce it to symbolic form, lay it at the doorstep of the subconscious mind, and await its interpretation. This process is helpful whenever a situation resists easy resolution, due either to its severity or its recurrence.

The purpose is to resolve a pressing life issue by understanding its deeper meaning, all the while "slipping it past" the ego. If you reduce a life challenge to symbol the ego assumes you are fantasizing, which it considers a pleasant diversion. Rather than worrying about a problem in its raw externalities—the abusive spouse, the depleted bank account, the ravages of cancer—the situation is rendered in broadly sketched caricature. While it sounds whimsical, in truth this makes it *easier* for the higher self to recognize and process the material, for at the higher levels of consciousness physical reality is an illusion. Rather than getting caught up in the minutiae of physical details, a cartoon image expresses its themes in broad strokes, making them more readily accessible to the higher self.

Using waking dreams also bleeds some of the raw, ego-fired emotion out of threatening situations. It is well and good to know that physical life is an illusion and you attract your life's experiences to you, but in the heat of battle—real or figurative—it is difficult to operate from this lofty awareness. Reducing a situation to cartoon imagery helps relieve the emotional intensity, dampening the ego's feline vigilance.

As an example, if you have a troubled relationship with your mother—who has never respected your impudent insistence on growing up, and who seeks to retain the tyrannical dominance she enjoyed when you were a toddler—rather than falling into familiar defensive patterns when she launches a tirade, reduce the scene to cartoon imagery. When that gleam of indignant rage flares in her eye, mentally step back and paint her in broad strokes: as a raging Tyrannosaur, a charging bull, a roaring bulldozer: whatever appeals. Picture yourself as a cowering rabbit, a trembling deer, a squirming worm. Laid bare, this is the dynamic of the relationship—predator-prey, dominance-submission—and by painting it in symbolic, cartoonish form, the higher self accesses that dynamic more directly.

It sounds fanciful, but the mechanism is valid: the ego's frantic defensive chatter is dampened since, after all, you are only watching a cartoon. This allows you to feed the event to the higher self in its immediately experienced intensity rather than later asking, in quiet meditation, for insight. The higher self evaluates its offshoots' experiences primarily in emotional rather than physical terms. Emotions are the signposts of your life's journey.

As another example, if you suffer from cancer you might visualize your body as a river and picture the tumor as a fallen tree or beaver dam: here, energy is blocked, stagnant, madly eddying in circles when it wishes to flow swift and clean. If it is possible to take a step back from yourself during chemotherapy or other treatment, you might picture the scene as wood nymphs and fairies helping to loosen the obstruction; you might say, "My body is a river but its flowing energy is blocked. What meaning does this hold?" The ego would welcome a pleasant fantasy of river and wood nymph over the harsh reality of chemotherapy, even as the imagery bypasses the ego-gatekeeper and soars to the higher self.

While a response may not be immediately forthcoming from the higher self—nor need it ever come explicitly—when used with some regularity the waking dream process opens a channel of communication among all levels of your being. The ego can relax, as it is entertained by fanciful imagery, while the conscious mind asks the higher self for guidance in understanding the deeper meaning of recurring or threatening events. By treating life's events as symbolic artifacts of deeper levels of consciousness—which, in truth, they are—all levels of the self can join in a rich communion which even the ego enjoys and benefits from. The result, at best, is a conscious awareness of the hidden meaning beneath life's perplexing events.

Our purpose has been to illuminate the processes occurring during dreamtime, and to offer suggestions as to how these processes can be consciously used to enhance the flow of communication from the higher self to the waking self. The key obstacle is the ego—which may claim to desire insight into life's deeper meaning but rejects anything hindering its pursuit of health, wealth, and love—and we have offered several techniques which consciously bypass the ego's vigilance to access deeper levels of consciousness.

Most important is the recognition that holding awareness of your life's deeper purpose, and the meaning of significant life events, will not *solve* your problems, merely illuminate them. They will no longer be esoteric mysteries, but dedicated effort is still required to resolve and release them. Your higher self stands ever willing to aid you in navigating your life's journey, and to do so with the clarity and vision your dream life offers you.

9

Meet The Metaphysical Beatles: Vanguards of the Revolution

[The Beatles] had an empathy and a kind of mind-reading business, such that when they were together they seemed to become another dimension.
Beatles producer George Martin

To understand the enduring legacy of the Beatles—whose music continues to move generations born long after their heyday—we must lay a cosmological foundation and work our way, step by step, to your everyday experience of art and its significance.

Music as Vibrational Information

Music can be understood as *information* expressed in symbolic vibrational patterns. The body carries the "key" to decode the information and absorb its meaning. Body and ears work in tandem: the ears perceive the musical stimulus and the brain judges whether it finds the stimulus attractive, neutral, or repugnant. This judgment is based on the degree of harmony between the body's vibrational patterns and the musical patterns perceived. Just as the body seeks out food, drink, and sex, the body also seeks out music which resonates with its internal rhythms, for the body is stimulated, reinforced, even healed, by immersion in harmonious musical atmospheres.

Because each new generation carries a distinctly higher vibrational "set point" than its elders—defining the boundaries of intellectual and spiritual potential—music is a primary medium through which a generation affirms and reinforces its shared essence. The music created and enjoyed by a generation is its communal "library" of knowledge and purpose that apprises them of who they are, reinforces the distinct tasks of their era, and offers a glimpse of probable futures down the road. One of music's most important effects is to bind a generation in a common vibrational pool, the better to harmonize its members with future vibrational shifts and with the larger sea of vibration in which the planet rides.

When we say music is information, what do we mean? We mean that, apart from any meaning carried in the lyrics, a musical melody is a pattern of tones expressing a concept; a packet of information. That information may be philosophical, emotional, or sensual; it may trigger new conceptual frameworks through which technological and artistic innovations arise; it may foretell future events; it may fulfill some or all of these purposes simultaneously. A musical pattern creates a vibrational atmosphere which entrains with any organism within its reach, apprising it of its subliminal message. The human body and psyche decode and interpret such messages, on levels subconscious.

Let us offer a hypothetical example. In a kingdom lorded over by a despotic, iron-fisted ruler, where protest meets instant execution and the long-suffering populace seems doomed to eternal privation, a young lad picking on a guitar "comes up with" a song that seems to materialize from the ether in a matter of moments. Its lyrics are nonsense of the tra-la-la variety, but the tune is fresh and breezy, uplifting and catchy, and soon everyone within earshot is humming and singing the song to themselves; quickly it spreads to captivate the village. This is of no concern to the king's fierce henchmen, who search instead for rabble-rousing radicals espousing democracy and equitable sharing of wealth.

What does the song say? On the surface, nothing; its lyrics are banal. Yet the melody carries the following information: (1) by universal law, a system that suppresses the aspirations for life, health, and freedom must ultimately fail; (2) the united efforts of powerless peasants can overcome the king's fierce machinery of repression; and (3) the king's jig is up, with a precipitating crisis soon to erupt. None of this is *consciously* available, to either the young songwriter or the village humming his catchy tune, but this information is *decoded* within the cells and psyche of every person hearing and singing it. Like a virus it spreads, stealthy and surreptitious, setting the stage for inevitable revolution. So a melody, an encoded matrix of information, spreads its meaning among all who hear it, preparing and fortifying their minds and bodies for impending social change.

(Of course many despots are well aware of the dangers art poses to authority; poets, writers, and singers are often the first on the chopping block.)

Musical Prophecy

One of the most important purposes of music, as we have seen, is that it can carry patterns not yet manifested in mainstream reality, the better to prepare a culture for impending evolutionary changes. In this sense, music is prophecy, vibrationally encoded prophecy. Does this mean that every piece of music carries the unabridged Future of Humankind embedded within its melody? Of course not. This brings us to a consideration of the process through which artists—in any medium—render their inspirations in tangible form.

Artists forge their creations through a marriage of *innate talent* and a clear connection to the spiritual realms, which we will call *communion*. Both aspects are necessary for an artist to successfully express his inspirations. Innate talent means a highly developed capacity for using one or more senses to forge tangible symbols of inner vision: an eye for color and perspective; a gift for poetical verse; an ear for musical tones and patterns. The ability to perceive and manipulate the symbols of an artistic medium, with greater power than common, is the mark of innate talent.

Many artists enjoy broad acceptance of their work while they are alive and creating, but their work fails to stand the test of time, fails to compel and inspire future generations. Other artists, the Great Masters, fashion works which remain seemingly immortal through time, embraced by centuries or even millennia of subsequent generations, in cultures far removed from their origin. What lies behind this broad range of ephemeral versus enduring works of art?

The difference lies in the degree of communion—the connection to higher spiritual realms—the artist enjoys. We might classify the range of communion as low communion, mid communion, and high communion. The very greatest artists, the Masters, enjoy the highest possible connection, perfect communion.

Everyday pop artists create from the low-communion level: they tap into the *extant* currents of society, the vibrations of the mainstream, and render them in symbolic form. Their creations are often catchy and pleasing, easy to digest and enjoy, and as enduring as bubble gum. Low-communion artists frequently enjoy great commercial success, as their output finds ready acceptance among the mainstream.

Mid-communion artists dive a bit deeper into the currents underlying society. They offer not only a symbolic digest of mainstream vibration, but flavor it with a tinge of future potential. Depending on the extent to which the artist favors substance over security, his work may appear dark, vaguely threatening, confusing, or offensive to the mainstream, even as it attracts and resonates with those on the cutting edge. Often these artists, torn by the tug-of-war between mainstream and higher energies, vacillate between them in their creations, offering some reassuringly mainstream works while interspersing them with less comprehensible products of deeper visions.

Artists enjoying high communion must live with the Cassandra-like irony of serving their culture so well as prophets, even as that culture often scorns or dismisses their work. For high-communion artists plunge headlong into the timeless realm of spiritual verity, swimming among probable futures swirling in the vast cosmic sea, and struggle to render their profound visions in tangible form using the tools and techniques of their day. They are rarely satisfied with their work, haunted by the gap between the vision and its manifested expression. Their works are often incomprehensible to the mainstream; they are frequently dismissed as lunatics or thrown in prison as vague threats to the social order.

Rarer still are artists endowed with the blessing and curse of perfect communion. These artists don't just bathe in the currents of spiritual truth and then return to everyday reality; they spend every moment of their lives suffused with such powerfully compelling visions, flowing directly from Ultimate Consciousness, that they know nothing else: they eat, drink, sleep, and breathe their art. Whatever task is at hand, their minds are always swimming with fresh impulses toward creation and they cannot rest until they wrestle them into form. Their work is both prodigious in output and blisteringly revolutionary in meaning. In all of modern history, perhaps a few dozen perfect-communion artists have graced the world, serving as beacons illuminating the culture's evolutionary path.

The Beatles as Soul Constellation

Almost all artists work solo: their creations are uniquely theirs, bearing the fiercely individualistic imprint of their private communion with the cosmos. The modern innovation of the rock group is an exception: the blending of disparate energies into a communal artistry of greater power and breadth than any of its members can achieve alone. While most rock groups are purely terrestrial in origin—that is, no prebirth agreement binds their souls—the Beatles were an exception. Here, an agreement was formed before their births to blend their disparate energies into a unified gestalt serving as the primary revolutionary trigger for the sixties.

Consider the western world in the fifties: rebuilding from the catastrophe of World War II—itself a holocaust of unprecedented savagery—and desperately needing a blast of fresh spiritual energy to restore the culture to the path of spiritual principle. Blacks, women, gays, etc., were all second-class citizens or worse, with the force of law and custom against them. The natural world was viewed as a vast strip mine, with oil for the pumping, wild game for the shooting, oceans for the plundering, and ore for the blasting. Western culture's core value of separation, which underlay its growth from its first days, now stood supreme in the fifties, with the holocaust of World War II behind and social and ecological catastrophes looming ahead.

The first principle of spiritual law is balance. A culture so egregiously off the rails of spiritual principle, so blind and harsh and life-toxic, must be restored to a spiritual foundation or collapse. A "trigger" was needed to ignite the revolutionary fires of incendiary social change; a trigger cleverly disguising its revolutionary force beneath a seemingly innocuous artistry: the better to mask its revolutionary import from the blinkered guardians of tradition. Most of the artists and activists spearheading social change would confront those guardians head-on and suffer the consequences; but before their earnest efforts could take root, the way must be cleared, the foundation laid, for spiritual revolution. The need was urgent for an irresistible force to wrest young people away from the values of their elders, to enlist them as foot soldiers of revolution.

The breadth of the required revolutionary change was so vast that one soul, however perfect its communion, would be hard-pressed to serve as the revolutionary trigger. To ensure that the audience reached would be as immense as possible, what might be termed the "Beatles soul constellation" was fashioned in the realms of spirit; that is, before birth its members agreed to participate and serve as the revolutionary trigger.

The Beatles soul constellation was to serve as the primary torchbearer throughout the initial period of revolutionary change. They would not only attract young people worldwide with their irresistible music; they would lead the revolution step by step— always a step ahead, paving the way, laying down the energies and portents of the future, binding the revolutionary generation in a communal embrace of shared purpose. To do so required a complexity, a tapestry of interwoven meanings and nuances, so their message would resonate as broadly and deeply as possible.

The primary dyad—John and Paul—formed the constellation's foundation. Theirs was a marriage of structure and artistry: while both were towering geniuses, Paul's soul nature was ordered, grounded, structured; he served as the planner, organizer, future-thinking half of the partnership. John's soul nature was more airy and ethereal, less rooted and rationally focused, more comfortable floating through clouds of inspiration. Together their blended energies formed a metaphor of the human experience: you are spiritual beings and you are physical beings. Thus the elemental essence of humanity was expressed in the Beatles' primary dyad.

More was needed, of course, for what lay beneath Western culture's malaise was spiritual impoverishment. A tired old religion, ossified into dogma and hostile to genuine mystical experience, had shrunk its followers' spiritual lives to stale ritual. Above all, what the culture hungered for was a fresh breath of spiritual illumination; liberating the primordial sense of wonder, awe, reverence, and direct communion with the divine.

Enter George. George's soul essence, though of the Innovator family of consciousness, was skewed strongly toward the spiritual soul aspect. Any good artist enjoys easy communion with the higher spiritual realms, but one whose soul is strongly aligned with spirit plunges straight to the heart of Ultimate Consciousness. This was George's soul nature—the bearer of spiritual verity—and despite the prominence of the primary dyad in the group's prodigious output, in fact John and Paul rode George's spiritual coattails to the heart of Ultimate Consciousness, there to drink from the very deepest wellsprings of inspiration. George provided a spiritual undercurrent, a gateway to the very depths of creativity, which enhanced the primary dyad's artistry.

This, then, is the essential arrangement of the Beatles soul constellation: a primary dyad expressing the hybrid essence of human experience—spirituality and physicality—suffused with a spiritual ambience enhancing the dyad's ability to reach the zenith of creative inspiration.

In truth it was not predestined that the fourth Beatle, the drummer, would be Ringo. What was needed was an anchor to the others' soaring inspirations; a sturdy foundation of mainstream energy and essence. Recall that perfect-communion artists often fail to reach the masses with their prophetic visions; thus there was a danger that the Beatles soul constellation, in its essential triad, would soar too high to captivate the mainstream. The drummer—providing the foundational rhythm beneath soaring inspiration—therefore needed to be solidly grounded, mainstream in outlook and temperament. As you may know, the core triad of the Beatles played together for years until bringing Ringo on board just before they "took off." Ringo's personality was more in harmony with the Beatles' overarching *positive energy*; they required a rhythmic foundation of upbeat, amiable, optimistic energy, and this they found in Ringo.

The Beatles as Revolutionary Vanguards

Nineteen sixty-three was the turning-point year, when forces and events aligned to trigger the sudden and dramatic cultural shift. Until this point, the Beatles had spent their working lives as a bar band, and while they were popular entertainers in this limited realm, they had shown scant promise of what was to come. For it wasn't until the revolutionary trigger was activated that the Beatles' soul essences could emerge, blend, and form the whole that was so much greater than its parts; a group soul-gestalt enjoying perfect communion with Ultimate Consciousness. In this year the agenda was finally put into play, and step one was activated: get their attention.

Youth is the age of deepest communion with the currents flowing beneath society and with the higher spiritual realms; the psyche is most plastic, flexible, and permeable at this age. Female consciousness skews toward the spiritual, while male consciousness

is more grounded. Thus it is no accident that when the Beatles began
fulfilling step one of their agenda, it was teenage girls—the most
intuitive age of the more spiritual sex—who felt the strongest pull
toward the irresistibly compelling energy of the Beatles. For while
the Beatles' songs at this point were simple love songs and older
rock standards, the *energy* produced by the group was of an altogether higher order. It said, to those who could hear its subliminal
message: A new day is dawning; a spiritual revolution is at hand;
join us and embrace the future.

Who could resist? Who among the super-intuitive young female
population could turn her back on such a sweet song of promise,
when parents and teachers offered such stale gruel by comparison?
And so the Pied Pipers worked their magic, loosening the ties
between generations, magnetically pulling their young followers
onto a new path, uncharted but glowing with promise. Young boys
began marching to this new drummer as well, both to impress the
Beatle-mad girls and because their young souls hungered for a more
genuine and authentic life than what their elders offered.

Within months after the dashing young American president was
murdered, a nation deep in mourning was witness to the Beatles' first
appearance. The fate of the old order was sealed: What young person
would submit to the hoary imperatives of old-guard custodians when
new myth-makers had arrived, so fresh and exuberant and full of
optimistic vitality? For this was the essence of the Beatles: a
relentlessly upbeat, sunny, hopeful zest for life. For the revolution to
appear attractive and worth the struggle, the fence-straddlers had to
be convinced that a better life, a life more authentically and happily
lived, would result from breaking ties with the old order and embracing the new. This the Beatles, with their seductively affirmative
energy, provided.

By 1965 the first step of the agenda was complete: the Beatles
had the world's attention. Now they could deepen and broaden the
message, imbuing it with subtleties and nuances, offering encoded
prophecy and poetry. Their musical repertoire broadened: for some
songs they traded the electric guitars for acoustic; others were
expressed through voice and orchestra. Their sophistication in the
studio grew as they struggled to find the closest musical expression
of their inspirations, flowing as they were from the heart of Ultimate
Consciousness. The rhythm of their music, previously a raw sexual

pulse, mellowed to entrain with higher levels of being, with the heart and mind and spirit. The first stinging strains of a sitar were heard as George, the mystic, introduced the Indian instrument as a symbolic forerunner of the flood of Eastern spirituality soon to wash through Western culture.

About this time the Beatles began experimenting with hallucinogenic drugs—a quick and powerful tool for shattering a staid and constricted consciousness—and weaving the fruits of their psychedelic visions into their music. Whether those listening were themselves moved to similar experimentation is beside the point: the Beatles provided it for them. The hypnotic, trance-inducing, no-chord song, "Tomorrow Never Knows," alters the consciousness of anyone within earshot, for the odd drum patterns, innovative sound effects, and entrancing vocal sedate the body while stimulating mind and spirit. The overtly psychedelic lyrics of "Lucy in the Sky with Diamonds" shatter established rules of language—newspaper taxis, marmalade skies, a girl with kaleidoscope eyes—just as LSD shatters the structures of the rational mind. By offering these hallucinogenic symbols the Beatles said: here, you see, it's all an illusion, reality is how you choose to construct it; if you don't believe us, try it for yourself! And a generation did.

By the time of the *Sgt. Pepper* album, not only was hallucinatory imagery permeating the Beatles' work, but the introduction of Eastern spirituality was made manifest with George's song "Within You Without You." Here was a dreamy, flowing river of poetry and music, a blend of Western and Eastern instruments, and one of the most blatant artistic prophecies in history: "And the time will come when you see we're all one, and life flows on within you and without you." At the height of their fame and fortune, the Beatles headed to India to study meditation, a journey whose impact continues to reverberate through an Eastern-inflected Western culture.

The Beatles' revolutionary impact was more than musical; it was cultural. Their appearance changed over time, always a few steps ahead of the mainstream, offering visual icons of prophecy. When they first appeared, they wore long hair, shattering traditional rules of male grooming. By their psychedelic period they wore clothes of fantastic design, color, and pattern; as if bits and pieces of fabric were tossed in the air and randomly sewn together—which is what they were doing, through their music, to Western culture:

tearing it apart and stitching the pieces back together in original patterns.

The End

Of course the Beatles did not *create* the revolution of the sixties; they served as the revolutionary vanguards for a much deeper process of cultural evolution. They rode the waves of transformation several leagues ahead of mainstream society, calling back in irresistible musical symbol the events and themes likely to unfold; but ultimately, as the revolution permeated every aspect of society, their role as vanguards was fulfilled. By 1967 the revolution was well under way as evidenced by nationwide protests against the Vietnam War; rising feminist, civil rights and environmental movements; the embrace of Eastern and native spirituality; sexual freedom; drug experimentation; and so on.

Between 1963 and 1967 the Beatles enjoyed perfect communion with Ultimate Consciousness; their blended energies soared to the very wellhead of creative and prophetic inspiration. Once their role as vanguards was fulfilled—the revolution was well under way and rolling forward on its own momentum—the deeper energies of cultural transformation shifted toward the next phase of evolutionary growth. The perfect synchrony between Beatle consciousness and the deeper consciousness guiding the process began to wane.

By the time the *Sgt. Pepper* album was released, the Beatles had fulfilled the first two tasks of their agenda: they had won the world's attention, then held it as they spun increasingly rich and esoteric tapestries of myth and song, weaving in imagery mocking the rational mind's limited scope, embracing the insights of the East. Though their communion with Ultimate Consciousness began to decline, this period saw creation of some of their greatest work.

By 1968 the energy of the Beatle soul-gestalt was waning. As always happens when the vitalizing consciousness suffusing an organism is withdrawn, the individual elements composing the organism are released to express their unique individuality, and decay sets in. This process afflicted the "organism" of the Beatles as their perfect communion with Ultimate Consciousness diminished. On a personal level, as they reached their late twenties, their focus shifted away from the Beatles' "group marriage" and toward fulfillment as husbands and fathers in families of their own.

Sensing this, they roused themselves for one final album and rode the crest of evolutionary energy, which buoyed them still, to create a masterpiece called *Abbey Road.* In the final song of the closing medley, appropriately titled "The End," the Beatles issued the world *their* marching orders: We've done our work, the old order is on the wane, the revolution is underway, be of good cheer, now we release you to the hard but essential task of building a new world. And they did so both as a group and as individuals: above the blistering two-chord rhythm, each member of the triad played a guitar solo, and the drummer his only drum solo, as a way of taking leave of the group and introducing themselves to the world as the independent musicians they would soon become. Their final words neatly expressed both the law of karma and their own experience as bandmates: "And in the end, the love you take is equal to the love you make."

That the Beatles' music should still be so popular—and that young people around the globe, who don't even understand the words, embrace their music—reflects two things. First, their perfect communion with Ultimate Consciousness means their music carries meanings so deep and complex that decades, if not centuries, must pass for mainstream society to catch up with their prophetic inspirations; just as you are not yet finished with Beethoven's visionary thunder. Second, the process of cultural transformation is long and hard and often ugly; despair, hopelessness, and resignation sap the energy of those struggling to forge a new order. What better way to refresh one's flagging vitality than by immersion in the musical atmosphere of the relentlessly joyful Beatles, the oracles of optimism, in messages ringing with hope and promise? For they peered far and deep into the future and their vision was crystal clear: No matter how challenging the road to cultural transformation appears, no matter how many obstacles the old-order guardians throw in your way, you can *take a sad song and make it better.*

Because the Beatles' role as revolutionary prophets is not recognized, neither are the many salutary developments their influence spawned. In the fifties the Western world was picking up the pieces of a shattered Europe. Today Europe is united, sharing a common currency and open borders; an unimaginable development 50 years ago. Revolutions in civil rights, environmental protection, women's equality, and gay rights are written into law—and enforced by the same cultural guardians who once furiously fought their enactment. Today's young people take such developments for granted; only old-timers can compare the new order with the old and shake their heads with wonder: how could so much happen in one lifetime? Because of the Beatles, whose revolutionary energy fed and led the transition from old order to new. Yeah yeah yeah.

10

Deep Astrology:
Swimming in the Cosmic Seas

As is the case in many aspects of life, "popular" astrology—with its zodiac signs, houses, cusps, and retrograde planets—is a facile, and easily understood, system hinting at a deeper reality. Like religion, it seeks to reduce the infinite and unknowable to a set of simple rules and principles by which humanity might live in harmony with the cosmos. Rather than assembling a pantheon of gods—or a God—to influence human affairs, astrology proposes that planets, stars, and other celestial bodies determine personality traits at birth and sketch the likely events unfolding in the future.

This is popular astrology, imbued with a certain fatalism both as to personal psychology (your birth sign locks you into certain characteristics) and life events (which are foretold by the stars). While readily dismissed by modern, educated persons, beneath the popular perception lies "deep" astrology, an ancient knowledge of the relationship between humanity and the cosmos, which gave birth, through millennia, to its popular stepchild. This knowledge has been honed by advanced societies spanning the globe and the millennia. Because deep astrology retains full vitality in the collective unconscious, it bleeds into awareness, however misshapen in popular form to conform with western principles of structure, hierarchy, and cause-and-effect.

The Cosmos as Energy Ocean

Because your eyes perceive the universe as a great black void punctuated by occasional planets and stars, you assume that the space between celestial objects is "empty." Given the western emphasis on sensory evidence as the arbiter of reality, such a perspective makes sense. It is, however, incomplete. Using "evidence of the senses" as the criterion for reality while employing only the five narrowly focused senses results in a fractured, partial perspective. What is missing is the "sixth sense" available to the species: the ability to perceive energy fields.

As with any human characteristic, there are many levels of natural skill, refined with training and focused study, leading to mastery in perceiving energy fields. The high priests of advanced societies were those born with heightened sensitivities, honed through years of disciplined training, resulting in exquisite sensitivity to the most minute shifts in energy, both local and remote. All members of such societies had at least a rudimentary sense of the play of energy around them, and this common awareness was the basis of their cosmology.

The difference between this cosmology and the modern western perspective boils down to this: you see empty space broken by occasional clusters of matter; they saw the cosmos as a pulsating ocean of energy—ranging from thin, vaporous mists to denser bodies of coagulated "matter." They saw that the ocean of energy washes through every form, no matter how seemingly solid; that even a stone is but pinpricks of thickened vibration dancing in a subtle mist. They saw how events occurring inches or light years away send ripples throughout the universe, bathing everything they touch with their energetic accent.

The universe was understood to manifest as two principal densities: mist and form. Mist is the ocean of vibration permeating the universe, the subtle carrier of energetic information. Energy pulsations travel most efficiently along strands of mist. Form is clusters of thickened vibration, the primordial "matter" of the cosmos. Because the human body is form, it hums at the same approximate frequencies as other such clusters, allowing humanity to perceive and manipulate its world.

For the adepts of advanced societies, the pulsating waves of energy washing through the universe were not simply "felt" by the body in a blind, diffuse way, but were also seen and heard. The body's energy sensors work in cooperation with the eyes and ears to weave a comprehensive picture of the vibrational waves flowing through its environs. With this heightened perception, sight and hearing expand beyond your present experience; as if three-dimensional sight and stereo sound ramify into richer, more complex vibrational patterns. At this level, the sharp distinction between sight and sound dissolves; sensory impressions blend with the body's energy sensors to weave a holistic energy-picture more felt than perceived.

A given field of energy can be perceived and manipulated from any number of perceptual focuses. Just as you might study an object by looking at it, sniffing it, tasting it, shaking it, and poking it to determine its nature, with multidimensional perception one can examine a vibrational field from a range of perspectives. An object-field can be beheld from any of the discrete senses' perceptions, or in combination, or enriched with the body sensors' subtle detection of fluctuating energy patterns. An object-field can be experienced solely as sound, as sight, as smell, as vibration; or in integrated wholeness. A great plasticity of perception is the hallmark of the adept. Those familiar with psychedelic agents may have experienced this multidimensional perception, though the scrambling of perception can be frightening to western brains unaccustomed to interpreting such richness of sensation.

In advanced societies possessing multidimensional perception, a wide range of perceptual abilities prevails. At the novice level, one may be able to perceive only the workings of one's own body: to detect a tumor, a nutritional imbalance, or an emotional wound. Moving up in the hierarchy of gifted and disciplined perceivers means a gradual expansion of perception, both in the distance at which events can be perceived and in discerning increasingly subtle fluctuations carried in mistborne vibration. The high priests are those from whom virtually nothing is hidden, for they perceive all: the thoughts and body states of those they meet; events occurring at great distances; even events not yet manifested, congealing toward expression in the swirl of probability.

Among the most sophisticated high priests, it was natural that they would seek to expand and refine their abilities by putting them to use detecting ever finer and more subtle vibrational fields. This meant leaving the earth plane entirely—for detecting its swarming fields, mist and form, came as second nature—and reaching further into the cosmos. Over time, as certain patterns of fluctuation were consistently linked with earthly events, and as cyclical cosmic patterns had observable effects on the bodies of those born during those patterns, the link between distant celestial bodies and human personality and experience became evident. This led, over generations, to a discrete field of study, available only to the most gifted perceivers, which grew into an elaborate system of cosmic-human influences, their timing and effects. This is "deep" astrology, the ancient foundation of today's popular stepchild.

One thing should be immediately apparent: Because the cosmic influences studied are so subtle, discernible only by the most advanced perceivers, they were understood to play a minor role in the development of personality and life's unfolding events. The rigid zodiacal signs of today's astrology, with their crisp lists of personality attributes and life forecasts, are but crude replicas of what was then understood as a more subtle and dynamic interplay between cosmic and human entities.

First of all, the moment of birth was not given the supreme importance it plays in popular astrology. It was understood that a growing fetus is constantly bathed in vibrational fields—the most significant being its mother's, of course, as well as her physical and emotional environment, her significant relationships, and so on. The moment of birth is important in that it involves the sudden expulsion from one vibrational environment to another: from the womb to the atmosphere. Whenever a body experiences such a rapid vibrational shift, it opens itself up to the energies of its environment as a way of quickly entraining to them and restoring symbiotic harmony between body and environs. This openness to external fields is never so pronounced as it is at birth.

This does not mean that Jupiter or the Big Dipper plays a formative role in the child's development. It means that distant and subtle cosmic events can impress themselves upon neonatal energy fields with a force they will not again have. Far more significant is the child's immediate birth environment. Babies in general, and newborns in particular, often cry until they are held because they feel "out of sorts" in their bodies: harmonizing a soul, a mind, a body, and its environment does not come easily. Babies anchor to human life by entraining to human energy fields, especially mother's comfortably familiar patterns.

The child's overall experience at birth is overwhelmingly shaped by the mother's emotional and physical condition, by the loving touch of others involved, by the immediate entraining to solid adult bodies. Into this powerful event, pulsing as it is with emotional and physical energy, the influence of distant cosmic bodies can be slight at best. For to the extent the infant's body seeks to entrain itself not only with its immediate environment, but with the universe at large, it is unusually receptive to imprinting by such influences. Let us explore how such influences operate.

The Cosmic Web

From your earthbound perspective, it is impossible to study the universe in its entirety and observe the intricate patterns of planets, moons, stars, and floating debris which form the "matter" of the cosmos. They appear as randomly placed, scattered clusters of suns, planets and moons. The Big Bang creation myth supports this perception of haphazardly placed celestial bodies, as all matter was supposedly spewed at random from the primordial explosion. We will not here address the Big Bang theory's creative fiction except to point out that believing in it hinders perception of the cosmos's true design.

The universe is eternal and without beginning or end, in the sense that it was not "born" and will not "die"; these are anthropo-morphic projections of your own mortality. Since ultimately all time is simultaneous, the universe has "always" existed as a venue of activity for bodies of consciousness seeking to explore matter-based existence. Like any physical structure, the universe must be organized into coherent, stable, self-sustaining patterns which endure through time, while allowing sufficient flexibility so as to weather the likely events and fluctuations inherent in the system. Thus, the placement of celestial bodies is not random, but follows patterns and principles ensuring the system's stability and endurance.

There are two basic types of celestial body: energy-absorbing and energy-releasing. We might call the former "sponges" and the latter "generators." All solid objects are sponges: planets, moons, asteroids, human beings, etc. They absorb energy from the cosmos in far greater proportion than they release it; they transmute cosmic and solar radiation into the building blocks of solid matter. Among sponges are variations based on the ratio of energy absorbed to energy released, their size, their constitution (rock, liquid, gas), their rotational velocity, the magnetic strength of their poles, whether their cores are solid or molten, and so on.

All energy-spewing bodies are generators: stars, for the most part, with an occasional exploding supernova or meteorite flaming to earth contributing fleeting energy bursts. Some generators are stable throughout millennia while others are a brilliant flash in the pan. The "temperature" of their radiation varies widely, as does the strength and consistency of their emissions (some steady and invariable, others explosive and random). All these factors influence the extent to which nearby objects can entrain with the generator's energetic shower.

Because the fundamental principle of Nature is balance, the universe as a whole, and its many smaller regions, must maintain balance between sponges and generators. Thus it is no accident that your sun is surrounded by planets, some with their own balancing moons, as well as several asteroid belts. A star must always be balanced by encircling sponges which absorb and neutralize the star's furious shower of radiation. A universe composed entirely of stars would soon vaporize. Each star's radiation must be contained within its local area and not spew into the universe at large, there to overheat other regions.

If you could build a three-dimensional model of the solar system, including the planets' gentle north-south rocking and their orbits around the sun, the relative positions of the planets and moons throughout the year, and the flow of solar radiation, you would observe a highly efficient and intricate system in which a generator is surrounded by a network of sponges which absorb and neutralize virtually all of the sun's radiation. Each planet, given its distance from the sun, absorbs a certain range of energy emissions, and uses its rotation and (with some) its north-sound rocking pattern, to prevent itself from being scorched to oblivion by the sun's fierce heat.

To elaborate on the range of energy each planet absorbs, every planet carries a certain density, a precise mix of elements in its body and its atmosphere, a unique size and volume, and a distance from the sun. These factors determine the range of solar radiation the planet can absorb. Solar radiation decreases in intensity the further it travels; thus, the closer planets are formed of rock and iron, absorbing highly stimulative energy, while the distant planets, largely liquid and gas, "mop up" the decelerating solar shower.

Most of the sun's energy spews from its equatorial region, along the plane where the planets lie. Solar radiation flowing from the poles tends to arc back toward the planets' gravitational pull; and what little escapes this pull is easily absorbed by the meteors and cosmic debris swimming through the system, acting as a kind of "floating sponge blanket." By the far reaches of the solar system, an average of 99% of solar radiation will have been absorbed by planetary, lunar, and other sponges.

The planets follow an intricately choreographed dance in which each is "aware" of the position and condition of the others; with an eye to maintaining the system's overall balance. If for some reason a planet is temporarily unable to absorb its quota of solar radiation, others will attempt to "pick up the slack" to the extent possible. This might involve a planet temporarily increasing or decreasing its surface temperature, or shading its color, to alter the range of solar radiation it can absorb. These changes take place over millennia— mere blinks of the cosmic eye—as the system works cooperatively to maintain balance and absorb all solar radiation.

Because your planet is unique in its blend of bedrock and water; can quickly expand its water-covered area with a flood or decrease it with a drought; and can shift its water stock from liquid to ice to gas with relative ease (over a few millennia in the case of an ice age); and because Earth's relative mid-point position is crucial to sustaining the balance of the solar system, Earth is among the most dynamic of the planets. The fierce electrical storms, volcanoes, earthquakes, floods, droughts, freezes, heat waves, ice and tropical ages—all the charming meteorological and telluric eccentricities which endear you to your cosmic home—serve both to maintain intraplanetary balance and contribute to stabilizing the solar system. It is unusual for a body composed largely of bedrock to know such constant dynamism in its surface and atmosphere, but the placement of Earth in the larger system makes it essential.

The Lunar Connection

Except for one of Jupiter's satellites, Earth's moon is the largest in proportion to its host planet of any moon in the solar system. This bespeaks the central importance of the moon in balancing and stabilizing Earth's vast liquid seas. The relationship between the moon and Earth permeates mythology and folklore, even if it is not rationally understood beyond calculating the rise and ebb of tides.

Earth's central problem is that it is bombarded with solar radiation, which it absorbs primarily in its bodies of water, and this radiation must be "organized" into fields of energy which can either be released to the atmosphere or dispersed through bedrock. The frenzy of solar radiation is such that the Earth's crust cannot offer a countervailing influence sufficient to decelerate and organize it; for one thing, there isn't enough crust to do the job; second, the crust is largely soil, which captures and absorbs energy less efficiently than rock. Left alone, this situation would lead inexorably to a dangerous rise in aquatic temperature, along with a fierce atmospheric electrical static precluding development of complex life forms.

Into this quandary rides the moon. The moon is solid bedrock, free of soil, with a virtually cold core (unlike Earth). Its function is to balance and organize the shower of solar radiation bombarding Earth. The rise and fall of the tides is like a great breath—inhale, exhale—as the moon helps arrange scattered solar radiation into coherent patterns. Since most such radiation is absorbed in bodies of water, here is where the moon's effect is most apparent. The moon suffuses Earth with a steady rhythm of tension and release—inhale, exhale—as the solar frenzy is captured and tamed in its rhythmic lunar cadence.

This process allows solar radiation to be "cooled down" to the point where Earth can effectively handle it. One of water's greatest strengths is its ability to disperse radiation rapidly and in all directions, minimizing its potential danger to life. Earth's crust pulses with a deep, steady rhythm, further slowing solar energy to rhythms compatible with life. What energy cannot be neutralized through water and bedrock is released to the atmosphere, where electrical storms flare without cease, dispersing highly charged energy with minimal risk to living beings.

The moon passes through a 28-day cycle of waxing and waning, during which it reflects lesser or greater solar energy onto Earth. In a sense, this reflected solar energy serves as an "attractor" to solar radiation swimming within Earth's seas, "beckoning" solar energy to entrain to its patterns. Because those patterns are heavily weighted with the moon's bedrock stability, solar radiation trapped in the Earth system is slowed and organized into quiescent, cohesive fields.

Chaos and Order

Essentially, the entire universal system boils down to the tension between chaos and order. This is the fundamental dynamic of any physical system, and it not only pervades celestial bodies such as planets, solar systems, and galaxies, but is the root dynamic of every life form. At a physical level, a species must have sufficient flexibility and spontaneity that it can break old patterns (chaos) and adapt to changing circumstances, but such flexibility must rest on a sturdy bodily structure (order) ensuring survival. At a cultural level, what are questions of liberty vs. dictatorship, war vs. peace, capitalism vs. communism, anarchy vs. fascism, liberal vs. conservative, marriage vs. singlehood—what are these deepest of human issues but expressions of a deeper dynamic tension between chaos and order?

Within the solar system, and the larger universe of which it is a tiny corner, the tension between chaos and order plays out on a grand scale. The sun is chaos—a fierce, blazing shower of incendiary radiation. The planets and moons are order—stable in their sizes, their orbits, and their cores, even as their surfaces play host to the eternal dynamic between chaos and order. The aim is balance: finding the proper mix of generators and sponges to ensure the system is continuously invigorated with fresh energy and yet stable enough to endure through time.

Planets and moons forge pathways of energetic communication across the solar system as a way of strengthening the sponges' power to neutralize solar radiation. Basic geometric shapes are often employed—circles, squares, especially triangles—as a way of transmitting and dispersing solar energy. The ancient game of playing "connect the dots" with celestial bodies, to discern their patterns, is not so far-fetched, for sponges and generators do the same. The shapes employed, and their relative sizes, change with the planets' rotations, bathing Earth in a dynamic energetic "atmosphere."

The essential meaning of the universe, then, is the dynamic interplay between chaos and order: finding the proper balance ensuring both stability and flexibility. Such a system operates most effectively when every element is apprised of information, both remote and local, which may bear an impact. Every planet "communicates" with every other planet, each with its moons, and all of them with the sun, the better to maintain the proper "mix" of chaos and order, generator and sponge, that sustains the solar system.

More distant cosmic objects and events play less of a role, but can be critically important if their energy "hits" at a time of temporary stress or weakness in the system. Mistborne vibration travels vast distances throughout the universe so the cosmic picture can be discerned at all times, however subtly.

Into this picture strolls the human race, standing atop a buckling, belching crust and below an atmosphere sizzling with storm and fury, on a planet whipping through day and night, winter and summer—and trying to make sense of it all. Like any form in this dynamic universe, the human body is exquisitely sensitive to the swarms of vibrational information bombarding it from near and far. We have seen that the newborn infant is especially sensitive to the influence of remote events and energy projections, yet such sensitivity endures throughout life. Let us explore this further.

Cosmic Geometry

When the astrologer-adepts of advanced societies turned their gaze skyward, they observed consistent patterns in the heavens which correlated with consistent patterns in human personality and events. One of the most readily observable patterns in the night sky, and one with apparently consistent effects on human life, was the complex energy matrices arising whenever celestial objects formed geometric patterns. The basic patterns are the line, the circle, the square (rectangle), and the triangle. Because the cosmos was perceived as an ocean of energy, its individual bodies were not accorded the importance they hold in popular astrology; rather, individual objects were seen to contribute characteristic ingredients to the greater cosmic soup. It is the soup, the blending of discrete vibrational flows into a richer stew, that impresses its patterns on all bodies within its sphere of influence.

The most basic relationship between bodies is the line, a simple flow between neighbors. The first factor defining a linear relationship is whether the flow is unidirectional or bidirectional. A unidirectional relationship almost always arises between a sponge and a generator: the sponge can only passively absorb the generator's fierce shower, offering but a thin vapor in response. The generator cannot perceive this slight responsive mist over its own cacophony. This is, indeed, the fundamental relationship in the universe: between an object generating energy and another absorbing that energy. A simple, one-way, straight line links these two objects.

Bidirectional relationships almost always arise between bodies of the same basic type: two generators or two sponges. It is rare for generators to share a strong two-way flow as the intervening sponges mop up most of their flow. At best, there might be a slight, regularly updated "awareness" of each other, like receiving a Christmas letter from someone with whom you share no real emotional connection.

It is between sponges, which are far more numerous, that genuine two-way relationships can develop. Such relationships can be classified, first, as either coequal or dominant-submissive (now the connection to human life becomes clear!). Bodies of similar bulk and constitution emit energies of relatively equal intensity; while between bodies of different sizes, the larger dominates its "submissive" partner, with a stronger flow of energy and gravitation. There is no real sense of power or domination involved here, simply the physical fact that a larger body emits a stronger flow of energy and greater gravitational pull than a smaller one.

A linear relationship is further defined by the nature of energy exchanged: either sympathetic or discordant. Sympathetic bodies share a mutually stabilizing core vibration. When one suffers a temporary fluctuation or weakness, the other offers a "helping hand" of restorative energy, pulling the weakened partner back to its native pattern. Discordant relationships are between bodies of markedly differing energetic qualities. The most obvious is between a sponge and a generator, but even among sponges the vast range of vibrational qualities ensures that some will clash and grate against each other.

Discordant relationships between sponges tend to weaken their energy fields. Particularly in relatively coequal relationships, where each gives as good as it gets, the constant bombardment by a foreign and discordant vibration forces protective measures which drain energy and stability. In a dominant-submissive relationship, the submissive partner suffers under the constant strain of trying to maintain its native energy under the ceaseless onslaught of inimical energies. Even the dominant partner suffers to some degree, as there is no reinforcing flow from the submissive partner: energy released is energy lost.

There are further refinements to relationships between sponges, but we will not delve into them here. The point is to recognize that the dynamic of "order versus chaos," which suffuses the universe and all its inhabitants, holds true for relationships between celestial bodies as well. A mutually reinforcing bond of common vibration strengthens and stabilizes both partners (order); while a discordant clash of antagonistic energies weakens them (chaos). From here, more complex relationships among celestial bodies arise.

The next step up in complexity is the triangle. Here, three bodies join in a tridirectional flow of communication. Each body shares linear relations with the other two, while subtly aware of the flow between its partners. Complexity arises because the three bodies may not lie in the same plane. The rhythmic waves suffusing the universe are built in "layers" of diverse qualities; bodies immersed in a given layer are imbued with its flavor. Thus, a triangle may contain three bodies lying in the same plane, two in one layer and the third in another, or all three in different layers. Communication across layers is more difficult than within a single layer; this complicates the original dynamic among the triangular partners.

As with linear relationships, triangles offer a spectrum of relationships, from the tight cohesion of three partners in the same layer sporting equal size and constitution; to the chaos of disparate partners in different layers engaged in an endless turmoil of dominance and submission. Here, two partners may "gang up" to offer mutual reinforcement while besieging the third; or one (particularly if a generator) may dominate the others, while the two submissives transmit reinforcing energy to each other.

(We should note that we are projecting anthropomorphic qualities of personality onto nonhuman celestial bodies simply to ease your understanding. There is no real "antagonism" or "dominance" among celestial bodies; we are simply describing the nature of their energy flows in familiar terms.)

Squares offer still more complexity in that, in addition to each body having linear relationships with two partners, there is a fourth partner with which a body has no direct contact. (Opposite partners could forge a direct linear bond, but then the "square" would devolve into two triangles!) The residue of the fourth partner's influence on the other two bodies may insinuate into their flows, but only as a subtle side effect. A four-way relationship multiples the possible combinations of relationship type: from four congruent, reinforcing bodies to a cacophony of dominance and submission.

The final elemental shape is the circle. Here again, partners could simply form linear flows between themselves, but there is a special strength derived from more complex constructions. A circle's energy can flow clockwise, counter-clockwise, or both directions simultaneously. Each body receives energy from its nearest sending body, flavors it with its own unique vibrational essence, and passes it along to its neighbor on the other side. Energy flows quickly and smoothly within a circle; a continuous rush of vibration. Circles are where the cosmos comes to dance.

Whatever the configuration among celestial bodies, the fields created among partners hum with the essence of their energies. The field inside a triangle racked by dominance and submission is choppy and unstable. The field inside a square of sympathetic partners is smooth and steady. The field inside a circle of blended sympathetic and discordant energies fluctuates dynamically between chaos and order.

Every celestial body is simultaneously engaged in many relationships. A given star, planet, or moon is a participant in linear, triangular, square, and circular relationships, all at once. The entire universe is packed with three-dimensionally overlapping relationships forged among far-flung partners. Further, as the fields within each shape blend or clash with intersecting fields, the cosmic soup becomes ever more complex. But we shall not delve further into this infinitely complicated universal architecture!

The Body Electromagnetic

What does this great cosmic stew of overlapping planes, angles, and fields have to do with you? The answer is that you are simmering in the stew at this moment, have done so since conception, and your life is inescapably colored by the flavor of the cosmic energies in which you swim. Your body is not merely the flesh and bone your senses perceive, but carries larger energy fields which form the complete "body." To break down another richly complex system into its basic structure, the three main layers of your energy fields are the memory field, the selfhood field, and the contact field.

Every physical occurrence—from a sneeze to an earthquake—results from the movement of molecules. This is the foundation of a memory matrix: a bundle of energy containing a record of molecular interaction (i.e., what happened?). In addition, thoughts and emotions, being expressed electromagnetically, are woven into the memory matrix of each event (i.e., what did you think and feel at that time?). This memory matrix, recording each moment of life, is encapsulated and held in the memory field, the field closest to the physical body.

The middle layer, the selfhood field, is where the higher self sculpts life task and life theme into energetic form. Incoming events are never perceived with pure, unfiltered clarity, but pass first through the selfhood field. Depending on its structure and tuning, some events will carry powerful impact while others pass through without a trace. The identical event is experienced in as many different ways as there are eyes (and selfhood fields) to perceive it. This "keeps you on track" by attracting you to events consonant with your life theme and steering you away from irrelevance.

The contact field is the vehicle through which you exchange information with those you meet and those you love. It carries a capsule summary of your life theme and tasks, reincarnational history, recent experiences, and so on. When you meet another, contact fields overlap and exchange this vibrational biography, the better for you to link with souls of like purpose and avoid those of an irrelevant or harmful nature. You hug those you love, especially after an absence, to ensure the highest-fidelity exchange of information.

Being of electromagnetic energy, these fields are exquisitely sensitive to the influence of other such fields. Even the distant relationships among stars and planets outside your solar system can be picked up in trace awareness, slight as their influence may be. And the dynamic, ever-fluctuating patterns and relationships forged among the partners within your solar system can carry significant effect indeed.

Natal Influences

As mentioned, the importance of the moment of birth has been vastly overstated in popular astrology. Since you swim in the cosmic soup from conception to death, choosing one particular moment as the "defining" one which marks you for life is simplistic at best. Still, the moment of conception and the time of birth can be pivotal points at which cosmic influences carry disproportionate effect.

Conception is significant because it is the moment when two cells—egg and sperm—fuse to forge potential new life. Until that moment, gametes are merely cast-off cells within their parent body; "cast-off" in the sense that they play no essential role in maintaining health. Their purpose is to beget the next generation, not to sustain the current one.

At the moment of conception, sperm and egg suddenly elevate their status from cast-offs to a new life form. The mother's body instantly knows conception has occurred and begins the all-encompassing shift to nourishing and sustaining the fetus. Larger influences also come into play, as souls hovering on the astral plane, searching for appropriate host mothers, become aware of a woman's pregnancy and evaluate her suitability. So conception, however private an event it may seem, generates ramifications at many levels.

The newly formed zygote has its own primary tasks: blending disparate genetic codes into a unique bodily template, multiplying its cells in a coordinated sequence, and entraining to the energies of its mother and her environs. This latter element is where cosmic influences may come into play. From the instant of conception—and until death—a living body seeks to entrain itself to its environment; to harmonize internal and external energies. This is especially crucial at conception, for a woman can be anywhere in the world—even on a boat at sea or soaring in the stratosphere—at conception. With some urgency, the zygote must entrain itself to its mother's environment as a means of stabilizing itself (since failure to stabilize often leads to spontaneous abortion).

Because the zygote urgently seeks stabilization, and because it is "wide open" to energetic influences from within and without its mother, any particularly strong cosmic influences can bear an impact. The moon, for instance, in its cyclical waxing and waning, offers a blend of stable and volatile energies. The fuller the moon, the greater the "chaos" in its beams as the sun's discordant shower is reflected in greater measure.

A new moon offers quiescent stability as its bedrock-flavored flow is not "excited" by the sun's random shower. A new moon therefore helps a zygote to stabilize and to "convince" it that the universe is a calm and ordered place; whereas a full moon's more volatile flow represents a chaotic, unstable universe. In very subtle ways, lunar influence can affect body consciousness for better or for ill and tip the balance between a stable, healthy body and one more susceptible to illness. Similarly, in the psychological realm, lunar influence may "tip the scale" between soundness and instability.

Another cosmic influence is the geometric relationships the Earth is involved in, either as direct participant or when simply floating through the fields of larger patterns. As might be expected, if such relationships are sympathetic, reinforcing the Earth's bedrock energies, they tend to enhance that stability. If the Earth passes through a phase of multiple discordant relationships (the cosmic precursor of the dysfunctional family), the Earth's energy is suffused with a theme of assault-and-defense and a general volatility. To the extent zygotes seek to entrain with the broader reaches of the universe, the degree of bedrock stability or cosmic disorder can influence the growing form toward equilibrium or imbalance.

It is important to note that these lunar and cosmic influences are, first, very subtle; and, second, bear influence only on zygotes experiencing difficulty in stabilizing. A zygote that from the moment of conception easily conflates its disparate genetic heritage and entrains to its mother is immune to external influence. Only an unstabilized zygote may—*may*—be imprinted with lunar/cosmic influence as it opens itself wide to universal energies, seeking to stabilize.

The single most significant effect is the relationship between sun and Earth, a classic example of a dominant/submissive relationship! The Earth can only strive to protect itself from the fierce electromagnetic shower streaming from the sun; it cannot answer in kind. The side of the Earth facing the sun is more or less in the sun's grip; though deflecting some radiation through the atmosphere and absorbing some in its oceans, nonetheless the Earth's sunny side must passively absorb the solar shower. You rise with the sun not only because you see better in daylight, but because your body is stimulated to action by the sun's dynamic energies.

Thus, conception is more stable occurring at night than in daylight. There is a reason why you tend to feel romantic and sexual in the evening rather than at noon: by making love then, with conception occurring within a few hours, the zygote has the rest of the night, while the Earth is restored to its native bedrock energies, to stabilize and entrain to its mother and the Earth. This offers a quiescent and anchoring energy to the freshly minted form. Conception occurring during daylight is instead suffused with the clash between solar and earth energies and the theme of dominance/ submission, a more volatile environment to which the zygote must entrain.

How significant are these influences? Very subtle. They are nuances, shadings and hues gently tinting the potential body, still blending its genetic codes and multiplying them into cells. They are more significant where there is greater difficulty in fusing two genetic backgrounds and stabilizing the zygote; where the parents are of different races, for instance, or come from different generations. As the genetic code is woven into a unique pattern within the zygote, a strong cosmic field of stable or volatile energy can influence, to a minor degree, the basic constitution of the body growing from that pattern, with ramifications for later health or infirmity, as well as basic personality traits.

Far more significant in forming the template of personality are the choices made by the higher self much further down the line. As a rule, no soul selects a fetus until at least the third month of pregnancy, as so many fetuses fail to survive to that threshold. Once a fetus passes that mark and appears viable, a soul can link with the fetus, blending its energies with the burgeoning form. Any cosmic or lunar influences on the fetal form would be noted by the soul and its higher self in selecting the fetus; and would be consonant with the personality and life themes planned for the life. In other words, the soul and higher self look for a fetus already bearing qualities consonant with the planned life theme, thereby reinforcing and building on any earlier cosmic or lunar influence. That influence is no more than a subtle background to the far more significant impact of the higher self.

For example, a higher self seeking an incarnation as a restless, rootless, rebellious iconoclast would do well to marry its conscious-ness to a form already suffused with volatility: where conception occurred at a sweltering noon followed by a full moon, all bathed in overlapping fields of discordant cosmic geometry. A higher self seeking to fashion a stable, ordinary lifetime would do better to find a fetus conceived in late evening under a new moon while the Earth floats through fields of cosmic concordance.

Some cosmic events play out in the universe's languid con-ception of time: where a cosmic instant grips the Earth for a human generation. The rise in the younger generation of attention deficit disorders, hyperactivity, psychological quirks and frailties, can to some extent be attributed to the rough cosmic seas through which the Earth has been sailing for the last few decades. There are larger forces at work with more direct responsibility, but subtle cosmic influences can "tip the scales" where a zygote hovers between stability and volatility.

In addition, because making a boy is more complex than making a girl—since all fetuses begin as female and males must make a hormonally mediated switch to maleness—boys as a whole are more susceptible to volatile cosmic influences as they pass through the complex process of gender conversion. The "boy" genetic pattern is also more unstable than the "girl" pattern because girls have two X chromosomes, each of which can compensate for flaws in the other; whereas boys, carrying one X and a lesser Y chromosome, lack this genetic backup. The result of all this instability is that male fetuses are generally more susceptible to cosmic influences, and are more strongly imprinted by them, for better or for worse.

After conception, the second milestone in a developing life is the time of birth. Here the nature of cosmic influence differs: unlike conception, where the zygote seeks to entrain itself to its universe, by the time of birth a fetus knows full well where it lives. The issue here is that the transition from an aqueous existence of constant temperature and unbroken darkness to an atmospheric environment of varying temperature and bright lights, along with the loss of mother's comforting heartbeat, is profoundly disorienting. Having been expelled from its blissful warm cocoon—in a cataclysmic, torturous wrench—the neonatal body is almost desperate to regain its lost stability by entraining to its new environment. Cosmic energies are one ingredient in the vibrational stew the newborn struggles to open itself to and entrain with.

The same principles hold here as with conception: while cosmic influences are slight, a highly volatile, discordant pattern can exacerbate a tendency toward bodily instability and illness; a stable, soothing pattern helps quickly stabilize the body. In cases where the neonatal body is already somewhat unstable, cosmic influences can be strong enough to "tip the scales" one way or the other.

Cosmic Personalities

So far we have discussed the effect cosmic influences may have on the body. What about consciousness itself, though, as expressed through personality? Is this also open to cosmic influence?

To an extent, yes. Since the higher self sculpts personality traits into the body's energy fields while it floats in utero, a strong cosmic influence can subtly imprint those fields. Again, because the fundamental dynamic of any physical system is the tension between chaos and order, this manifests in personality terms as stabilizing or destabilizing effects. Traditional astrology often posits four main personality types aligned with the four elements: fiery, earthy, airy and watery signs. This has validity in that the tension between chaos and order is expressed in personality terms as the volcanic hotheads (fiery), the stable but dull (earthy), and those in between (airy and watery). Where a cosmic influence is particularly strong, or where the nascent personality template is unusually receptive to outside influence, cosmic energies can "tip the scales."

However subtle, the state of the cosmos always leaves an imprint in the personalities of those born at a given time. Because the body is an electromagnetic entity, exquisitely attuned to the state of its environment, it feels most alive and vitalized when cosmic conditions later match those extant during conception and birth. An extra "push" of vitalizing energy resonates within the body during such periods of cosmic consonance; one feels more at home in the world. Conversely, cosmic and lunar influences can grate and clash against the body's energy fields, making one feel out of sorts. It is well known that jails and asylums roil with turbulence during the full moon: naturally, for already unstable personalities are further destabilized by chaotic solar energy reflected in full measure by the moon.

The notion that cosmic influences mold personality at birth, or that they dictate life events, is simplistic fatalism. Cosmic influences are too subtle to wield such power. Nonetheless, they do subtly imprint themselves at conception and birth, and later affect one's overall feeling of comfort or discomfort as Earth passes through shifting phases of cosmic influence: life just "works" better when the cosmos is aligned with conditions similar to those extant at your conception and birth.

Toward a New Astrology

To this point we have refrained from describing cosmic influences in popular astrological terms: delineating signs of the zodiac, ascribing personality traits to planets, granting signal importance to the moment of birth, weaving a tapestry of houses, signs, cusps, retrogrades, etc. There are three reasons why such a system falls short: one, it grants too much importance to individual celestial bodies; two, it forces cosmic rhythms into the earth-year calendar, a gross distortion; three, it breaks cosmic influences down too finely and distinctly, as into the twelve zodiac signs, each with its unique characteristics.

While we would not presume to offer a comprehensive astrological cosmology to replace popular notions, we can offer a few principles as a restatement of ancient wisdom. A "deep" astrology would be founded on these principles:

1. In order of importance, the influences on personality and life events are: higher-self and soul choices; mother; family, culture, and environment; Earth, sun, and moon; other cosmic influences.

2. The foundational principle is that the primary dynamic of the universe is the tension between chaos and order. Cosmic influences are not so specific that they dictate personality attributes like the "stubborn" Taurus or the "diligent" Virgo. Rather, cosmic energies may influence personality by stabilizing or destabilizing the body's energy fields, pulling them toward chaos or order. Only an unstabilized fetus is susceptible to such cosmic influences.

3. Principal astrological "types" fall into these categories: earth types, sun types, water types, space types, star types. Earth types resonate with the Earth's and moon's stable, languid energies. Sun types fulminate with erratic, dynamic energies. Water types synthesize earth and sun types: reflecting water's dynamic motion and adaptability as well as its deep tranquility. Space types are those (rare) souls highly attuned to cosmic events, who feel fluctuating cosmic energies as acutely as night and day. Star types carry stars' dynamic and volatile energies but encased within a stable shell, tamed and well controlled.

4. An astrological chart of the highest accuracy would require information both from the moment of conception and the moment of birth. In advanced societies, where the importance of knowing the time of conception was recognized, women developed acute

sensitivity to the time of conception and could feel the body's sudden shift to maternal alertness. Factors to be considered would include time of day (night or day), phase of the moon, season of the year, latitude (as the angle of the sun's rays affects its influence), geologic setting (where conception took place), and whether powerful cosmic fields were then affecting the Earth. Similar information would be gathered for the time of birth. This information would be synthesized into a chart, forearming the parents with an educated estimate of cosmic influences on their child's personality and life path.

5. Cosmic geometry was studied meticulously and constantly. Some patterns and constellations exist for moments, others for millennia. Gone is the simplistic earth-year chart with its zodiacal divisions. In its place, a more complex and dynamic tracking of cosmic events and geometric constellations, and their effects on Earth, was developed. This required the insights of highly skilled energy sensors who could detect the minute vibrational effects of distant celestial events. By tracking these events; the shape, size, and distance of celestial constellations; determining the nature of their energy fields and angles to Earth; and the more obvious solar, lunar, and planetary influences, a sophisticated holographic picture of the cosmic "soup" in which the Earth floats could be determined for any given moment. Meticulous records were kept, and over time certain patterns emerged which seemed to have consistent effects on human personality and life events.

6. The predictive power of this information arises from the fact that any individual's astrological "type" can be charted, and the Earth's travels through fluctuating cosmic fields can be predicted with fair accuracy. Thus, there are anticipated periods of "congruence with the universe" and other phases of "discordance with the universe." Naturally, one would focus on making major decisions, changes in life direction, and holding reins of power and leadership, during one's "congruent" phases. (In such advanced societies, leaders would serve only during their "congruent" periods, stepping down as shifting cosmic patterns disfavored them.) One would be advised to lay low and refrain from major decisions and life changes during periods of discordance. One could thus chart one's life "in advance," with fair accuracy, knowing when the cosmos would be likely to reinforce and stabilize, and when to besiege and destabilize.

Of course there are infinite complexities we have not touched upon here. Our point is not to restore deep astrology in its full comprehensive glory—that would require volumes—but to introduce you to the ancient wisdom of which today's popular astrology is but a faint echo. The overarching principle of deep astrology is that, while cosmic influences are genuine, they are also subtle. They do not indelibly mark the personality at birth, nor do they rigidly determine the course of life. Still, an awareness of cosmic influences can be helpful in understanding oneself and charting the most effective and fulfilling course through life. It is to be hoped that such a system may again arise to replace today's simplistic popular astrology, and restore you to your true and proper relationship with the cosmos.

11

From Scalpel to Song:
The Future of Healing

As your culture passes through a transformational shift affecting every aspect of society, one of the most promising trends is in the field of medicine. Let us retrace the steps of western culture's medical development, beginning with the philosophical and scientific building blocks of traditional medicine, and project the developments to unfold in the future.

Phase One: The Sinful Machine

In the Judeo-Christian tradition, the body is viewed as inherently sinful, carrying the stain of the Original Edenic Sin. For many centuries, the medical profession (such as it was) unconsciously accepted and operated from this perspective. Luther, the Enlightenment, and the Scientific Revolution placed scientists in an increasingly uncomfortable conflict between religious dogma and scientific findings. While some centuries passed with scientific minds struggling to balance faith and reason, the point came when the chasm between dogma and discovery grew so wide that consideration of any spiritual influence on the workings of the natural world had to be abandoned. God and His miraculous seven days were summarily shown the door of the zeitgeist, and the Big Bang ushered in.

For the last few hundred years the "body as machine" model has dominated the western approach to medicine and healing. Surgery and drugs are the tools of choice in repairing the body-machine when, like any mechanical device, it breaks down. No consideration has been granted to the sufferer's state of mind, environment, family and emotional life, and so on. This model has often been spectacularly successful in diagnosis of disease—determining the nature and origin of illness—but falls far short in stimulating and working with the body's natural healing abilities or encouraging the sufferer's active participation in the healing process.

The limitations of the body-as-machine model have become increasingly apparent—the influence of mind, emotions, and love on health and healing increasingly recognized—nudging medicine toward its next phase of development, holistic medicine.

Phase Two: Holistic Medicine

Throughout western culture, old cultural and scientific models are being superseded by deeper, richer, subtler paradigms grounded in *holism*. Holism, as a worldview, posits that living beings are more than the mere sum of their parts (the machine model); and that consciousness and spirit (free of religious dogma) are inextricably woven into the total being, whether plant, animal, or human. In medicine, this means recognizing the "whole person" as an indivisible gestalt of mind and body; granting consciousness, however elementary, to the cells and organs; and considering the emotional/physical/spiritual environment in which a body dwells as a primary influence on its health or disability.

Merely granting consciousness any influence at all represents a major step forward, for it replaces the machine model with a subtler perspective in which the body is animated by consciousness flowing from the mind and (some would say) from the spirit or soul as well. When meditators were able to lower their body temperature at will, the machine model had to be updated, its scope broadened, to allow for the subtle interplay between cellular consciousness and the mind's higher consciousness.

While it seems second nature to you now to consider psychological and emotional influences on the body, this recent development, which is still being "worked out" through experimentation and clinical observation, broadens the picture to allow mental and emotional states to affect the body's health. Broadening the picture still further is consideration of the larger environment—both its overt influences such as toxics and stress, and the more subtle effects of noise, personal relationships, and the larger networks, such as neighborhood and community, in which one dwells.

All this broadening of the traditional machine model of the body results in *holistic medicine*, which rests on a respect for the oneness of mind and body; the subtle but powerful effects of consciousness on matter; the influence of external agents, both physical and psychological, on one's health; and the recognition that the human body is not a self-contained, isolated unit, but is embedded in a web of connections and relationships bearing heavily on one's physical and emotional health.

This is holistic medicine; and, as we mentioned, the philosophy, ramifications, and techniques of this new approach are still being explored in a number of disciplines. A widely accepted medical doctrine rooted in holism still lies some time in the future.

Phase Three: Vibrational Medicine

As promising as holistic medicine is, and however great its theoretical leap from the machine model, it still represents but a step forward on your progress toward a radically enlightened medical philosophy and practice. It is human nature to evaluate new ideas through the prism of the extant worldview; thus, holistic medicine must prove itself through validation by the experimental method of science. This validation is hindered by the relative crudity of instrumentation available in medical research, especially with regard to the body's subtle energies; and science can't define or measure consciousness at all, placing an artificial limit on its experimental reach.

It is like watching a movie on a tiny handheld screen, or listening to Beethoven through cheap car speakers: in both cases the original creation is diminished for passing through a lesser medium. Similarly, the body's subtle energy flows and minute electrical activity pass undetected by instruments unable to perceive or measure them, and pure consciousness cannot be perceived at all.

So, although holistic medicine is a step on the path toward a more comprehensive medicine, it is but a step. Beyond holistic medicine lies *vibrational medicine*, a philosophy and practice of healing rooted in the awareness that the body is essentially energy, energy sculpted into a complex network of patterns manifesting as the various organs, tissues, and so on. Sound and light, being also energetic fields of vibration, are understood to interact with the denser energy patterns of the body and to stimulate healing when properly applied.

Because this field is in its infancy, and because scientific validation lies years away, we offer here a brief overview of the basis of vibrational medicine, the energetic blueprint of the body.

The Body Electric

In deepest terms, the body's blueprint lies outside the physical system. Every living being, plant or animal, springs from a nonphysical blueprint which pulses in and out of physical existence. Your senses cannot perceive this near-instantaneous blinking "on" and "off"; your mind leaps the gaps of "nonexistence" and paints a sturdy picture of endurance and stability. (As an analogy, when you watch a movie in a theater, the screen is black between frames; but your mind leaps the gap and weaves an illusory "motion" picture.)

This blueprint is not simply a mirror image of the body, for it contains every potential form the body assumes from conception through old age. The blueprint is a bank of probabilities, then, which will be sequentially actualized and thrust into physical manifestation in accordance with the rhythms dictated by a species' developmental template and each being's private purpose. The blueprint can thus be thought of as a "master body," from which each moment of a body's growth springs in exquisitely detailed and precise form.

The human blueprint follows a standard template for the body's growth and maturation, and thrusts into physical form with each new pulsation precisely the "coordinates" required to advance the body's chronological age ever so slightly. These coordinates can be thought of as pinpricks of magnetic energy whose patterns precisely mirror the energetic patterns of earth elements.

You understand earth elements on the periodic table as having varying numbers of subatomic particles configured in a variety of patterns which distinguish their nature and behavior. Beneath these subatomic elements lies an energetic blueprint which dictates the size, shape, and pattern of each element; which we might term the "element" blueprint. A living being's blueprint, then, is a tapestry of such elements woven in precisely configured patterns which, when thrust into physical existence, magnetically attract earth elements into place.

In other words, a three-dimensional gridwork is thrust into physical life, each minute point of which pulses with the vibratory pattern of a given earth element; earth elements are thus attracted into place and held there by the magnetic force of the blueprint. Earth elements take their place in the body's form as directed by the blueprint; and when one element "dies"—for the stable life of these minute elements is quite short—an identical element will be pulled into place. Thus is the continuity and stability of the body maintained even as it constantly sloughs off its subatomic and cellular elements.

The "glue" binding these elements together is consciousness. The blueprint is not simply thrust into physical reality as an inert set of instructions, but is embedded in a matrix of consciousness apprising each earth element of the immediate structure it is contributing to, the larger structure (the body) of which it is a part, the purpose of the individual life, and the species of which the body is a member. In addition, a living being's consciousness feeds a constant stream of information down to the cellular level, apprising the cells of environmental conditions and other developments; this information is then impressed, in attenuated form, down to the earth elements.

A living being's thoughts and experiences thus blend with the consciousness carried by the blueprint to create a blended matrix of consciousness infusing every corporeal element. This stream of information—from physical and nonphysical realms—maintains the body's integrity over time. Here is where your private beliefs about health and aging can affect the body's blueprint—as your thoughts are blended into the matrix—and attract sympathetic events of health or illness toward manifestation.

There is no level of physical reality at which matter is not "alive," possessing consciousness and communicating with the larger networks in which it is embedded. Certainly the consciousness of an electron would seem irredeemably dim were you able to perceive it, but each level of material complexity carries a consciousness commensurate with its purpose.

With the understanding that the body is not so much "cells and organs" as it is matrices of consciousness and matter of varying complexity; that these matrices arise in the nonphysical realm and pulse into physical existence; and that each level of bodily complexity carries a commensurate degree of consciousness, the foundation of vibrational medicine is laid.

Vibrational medicine rests on the fundamental law of Nature: balance. When two vibrational fields intersect, their "differences"—in temperature, density, energy, etc.—tend to compromise toward a balanced synthesis. When you open a door between a hot room and a cold room, you get two lukewarm rooms. Nature always seeks balance, disparity yielding to synthesis.

This principle informs vibrational medicine's principal tools, light and sound. If an area of the body suffers from depressed or scrambled energy patterns, entraining the afflicted area to a field of similar vibrational pattern, *especially of a higher frequency*, spurs the weakened area back toward health and balance. It is vital that the energetic patterns used to effect healing be of a higher frequency than the body's, for the urge toward balance encourages a compromise between fields of varying intensity. Thus the body "accelerates" to entrain with a higher-frequency field, and in so doing hastens its recovery.

As a simple example, which would you prefer when arriving home in a rainstorm, soaked and chilled to the bone—a bathtub full of lukewarm water or steaming hot water? You naturally choose the hot water, because your body will "compromise" with its heat and bring your body temperature back to equilibrium much more quickly than soaking in lukewarm water would do. At the same time, your body's endurance for hot water is limited because once comfortable warmth is achieved, the heat continues to urge your body toward still higher temperatures, beyond the body's comfort zone.

The use of sound and light in vibrational medicine reflects this understanding—light and sound being vibrational fields of a frequency above the body's rather dense vibration. On the one hand, this ensures that light and sound will stimulate the body toward an accelerated frequency; on the other, if the difference in frequency between the body and vibrational fields is too great, the body cannot entrain to the higher patterns and no compromise can occur. The body's cells turn "deaf ears" to frequencies outside their perceptual range.

Vibrational medicine must therefore be grounded in a precise knowledge of the vibrational patterns of the body's cells and organs, and the allowable "gap" between the frequencies of body and therapeutic fields. As sound vibration is of a slower frequency than light vibration, initial experimentation would be focused in this area as results will come more quickly and faithfully.

Your everyday experience confirms this. Consider the disparate intensity of your mental and bodily reactions to the art forms of music versus painting. Do you react with the same passionate like or dislike to classical music as to Cezanne; rock and roll as to Monet; heavy metal as to Rembrandt? Is the strength of your visceral attraction or repulsion to rap or reggae or Mozart matched by equal intensity toward impressionists or cubists? Does purple trigger the same response as jazz?

Our point is that sound vibration, being much closer to the body's frequencies than light vibration, entrains more readily with the body and therefore triggers stronger reactions as the body is "pulled" toward harmonizing with the musical patterns, or actively resists entrainment with discordant sound. Light energy hums further from the body's vibrations, entrains less easily with them, and thus triggers comparatively subdued responses; although, curiously, your species is wired to favor sight over sound in everyday life.

Visible light and audible sound are two narrow bands of the vibrational spectrum. A further refinement of vibrational medicine, then, would be to explore and harness the energies lying outside those frequencies perceptible to your senses; for you swim in them from birth to death. Doing so would require development of instruments which can render such frequencies in visual or auditory fashion, enabling you to manipulate them. We will not explore this idea further here, only mention it as a broadening of vibrational medicine beyond its foundation in sight and sound.

From Cave Man to Vapor Man

Central to our discussion is the understanding that the human experience through time rides atop a gradual acceleration of Earth's core frequency, which in turn slowly accelerates the body's core energies. As the body accelerates, it becomes less dense, less bound to matter, and therefore nudges closer to the frequencies of sound and light. Vibrational medicine glimmers at the horizon of medical potential because your bodies have not yet accelerated to the point where such treatments offer consistent, reliable results.

As is often the case in your age of turmoil and transformation, you stand on one side of a chasm, surrounded by the intellectual and religious artifacts of your heritage, spying the gleaming hints of potential enticing you from the far side, yet finding no bridge offering an easy crossing. Yours is an age of sudden transition from one worldview to another, and the incremental steps of social evolution have been compressed into one great leap.

In medicine, the shortcomings of the western tradition have become glaringly apparent, yet no refinement has arrived to universal acceptance. Instead, fragments of potential glimmer from across the chasm, but because their time has not yet come—the Earth has not accelerated to allow their full expression—they remain maddeningly inconsistent, offering miraculous cures in some cases and failing in others.

Thus, it is for future generations to make everyday use of vibrational medicine. When the human body has accelerated to the point where its vibrational frequencies pulse closer to those of sound and light, the results will be more powerful and reliable. Still, much progress can be made in your time toward drawing that promising potential closer to manifestation.

Sing For Your Life

One of the most powerful tools of vibrational healing is the human voice. Given that there must be "overlap" between vibrational fields for communication and synthesis to occur, it stands to reason that sound frequencies emanating from the human body will naturally entrain with other bodies. Not only is there an automatic sympathy of vibrational frequency, body to body, but because the "consciousness source" of the sound is another human body, the consciousness of the receiving body is able to link with it at all levels—the denser corporeal level and the higher consciousness level. Since every grid-point of your body carries both a physical frequency and consciousness, the richest bond will be with vibrational sources of sympathetic "matter" and "consciousness" patterns.

This was known to many cultures, among both ancient civilizations lost to time and contemporary indigenous peoples. When shamans and healers sing while they work, they use deliberately crafted pitches, tones, and pauses to mimic healthy vibrational patterns of the afflicted area. This "rounds out" the healing power of substances such as herbs applied to the afflicted area, for while a physical substance entrains with the body's cells, the shamanic song entrains with the body's consciousness. This is a multileveled, powerfully comprehensive approach to healing.

Even more powerful than a single human voice is communal singing. Among ancient civilizations, such healers would work by sitting a dozen to a circle with the sufferer lying inside the circle. Through exquisite control of breath and pitch, invisible matrices of vibration would be woven around the afflicted; powerful clouds of song invigorated the body while the loving intent carried on the breath stimulated vitality and a lust for life.

In turn, these song healers took their cues—literally—from the songs of the cosmos, which they perceived in meditation. Each individual in the group tuned to a planet, the moon, the sun, or a gurgling waterfall, and brought forth in vocal form the equivalent vibrational patterns. Thus all of the elements of physical life—the cosmic, telluric, solar, and lunar energies—were woven in song carrying the force and imprint of the entire universe. How could the body *not* respond with vibrant health to such a cosmic symphony?

In your time, with the emphasis on external agents as healing tools, and the deprecation of native wisdom, the power of song in healing has been lost. Yet, as with any other potential, it lies latent in full vitality, awaiting a spark of interest to resume its place in the healing repertoire.

Your technological sophistication allows you to build on the principles of "song healing" and evolve an even more elaborate, sophisticated, and accurate system of healing with sound. As instruments of sufficient sophistication are developed, the human body can be "mapped" as a grid of vibrational patterns, each organ or fluid singing in a unique voice. These vibrational matrices can be precisely duplicated in digital form, and the body immersed in a sonic cocoon of healing energy.

A healing session consists of more than exposing the body to an appropriate vibrational pattern and frequency for the proper duration. Like a symphony, a healing session states its theme at the outset, builds and elaborates on that theme, and then soars to conclusion. A "sound healing" session would be similarly constructed, in that it would begin by individually stimulating discrete elements of the afflicted area, gently arousing them to receive healing, then follow with an integrated sound pattern blending all frequencies of the afflicted area. When the body has reached its limit of absorption of this sonic symphony, the sound would gradually taper off to gently "put to rest" each discrete element by sounding its pitch in gradually decreasing volume. A sound healing session thus begins softly, rises to a crescendo of invigorating stimulation, then tapers off to a whispering coda.

By the time such technologies are feasible, your ability to digitally capture the human voice will be so refined that sound healing will still be transmitted on "human" breath, though programmed and delivered by computer. The importance of human touch will never be lost, and a new breed of healers who touch the patient during sound healing sessions and blend their voices with the sonic symphony will serve as the heart of the process.

This is one strand of sound's potential for healing, one of many. What of using light, then? Again, because light sizzles at a higher frequency than sound, your ability to harness it for healing, and the body's capacity for entraining with it, are less than for sound. Still, as the human body accelerates over time, light will become increasingly useful as a healing tool.

The vibrational energies emitted by the body's cells not only "sing," they glow. While invisible to all but the rarest of eyes, the body's energy fields emit a constant stream of radiation. This radiation largely lies outside the visible spectrum, yet it carries filaments inside that range. These are so slender and attenuated that they pass undetected by all but the psychically gifted. These energy patterns carry profound clues as to the health and vitality of the body. As with sound, each organ and fluid of the body glows in a distinct hue when healthy. Instrumentation (or a trained psychic eye) can evaluate this radiant information and detect disturbances in the body's health and vitality.

Because light is so much more powerful an energy than sound, it must be applied sparingly and skillfully. A "light healing" session would begin in darkness, then gradually envelop the body in a pure white glow. White is the blending of all colors, providing the foundation by stimulating the body to a generalized higher frequency. Then the afflicted area of the body would be bathed in a precisely balanced blend of light frequencies carrying the healthy patterns of the area. The intensity would be just a notch higher than the extant energy, gently stimulating the body but not overwhelming it. Warmth, not fire, is the healer's tool.

Another "light" healing tool is already in use to some extent: lasers. These precisely focused beams of light can perform "energetic surgery" which, while still intrusive, is much less so than the scalpel. At present this tool is crude, and its potential includes a far more sophisticated matrix of laser beams blended to entrain with a damaged area of the body. Because of its intensity, such an application would be used only in cases of severe trauma to the body, where the tissues are so damaged that they have virtually no innate spark to start the healing process. A laser-grid application can "jump start" such healing, after which the less intensive "light healing" discussed above would be employed.

Embracing Your Healing Potential

A discussion of high-tech potentials for healing with light and sound may excite and delight you, but it may also leave you despairing, living as you do in the era of scalpels and pharmaceuticals. Let us close, then, by affirming that you have at your disposal the most powerful healing technology ever to be known: the human body.

When you consider that healing is best effected when an afflicted area comes in contact with a similar field of healthy energies; and when the consciousness of the afflicted area is stimulated and invigorated as much as its "matter," then what higher, more precise form of healing could there be than sharing close contact with one who loves you? For here, where skin meets skin, not only do parallel fields of energy overlap, thus entraining the wounded "matter" to its healthy counterpart, but the consciousness of the two bodies flows on mutual love.

This is not to suggest that severe, chronic, or terminal illness can be cured with a hug—rather, it emphasizes the importance of regular affectionate contact for the purpose of *preventing* such conditions in the first place. When you share your life and space with a long-term partner, your discrete energy fields entrain so completely that they create a hybrid energy form, a "couple" vibrational field, which can nourish either partner *in the physical absence of the other.* Thus, your partner can send healing energy to you from a great distance, for you are able to drink from the hybrid energy field enveloping you both.

Your culture is just now beginning to recognize the importance of touch and affection in maintaining physical and emotional health; and the deleterious effects a lack of affectionate contact has, especially on children. Little experimentation has been done in this area, given the crudity of available instrumentation. Far in the future lies an evolved medicine utilizing the ability to perceive the body's energy fields at will; where healers envelop patients in healing energy precisely directed to areas of incipient or manifest illness. Of course this process also rides on the deeper evolution toward developing "light bodies" increasingly freed from the limitations and density of matter.

As your species evolves, its focus will be less on employing earthly life as a primarily *material* realm of experience, and more on adventures in consciousness gently rooted in physical life but not tightly bound to it. Thus, the emphasis so many place today on using their bodies as vehicles for learning and growth—through sickness and in health—will be forsaken in favor of enjoying the body as a gentle feedback instrument reinforcing the lessons learned in spiritual, mental, and emotional experience.

When this stage of human development has been reached, the whole medical establishment will be sloughed off, for an understanding of the body's design and healthy functioning, and the power to heal incipient illness through love-focused touch, will largely obviate the need for dedicated healers. Beyond vibrational medicine, then, lies *conscious medicine* in which one's awareness of one's body—and others' bodies—is so thorough and richly detailed that no ailment could far proceed before being detected and cured either through private affirmation or the loving touch and song of another.

As always, fragments of the future tumble backward in time to prepare your species for growth. When you sing a child to sleep with a gentle lullaby, when you croon romantic verses to a loved one, when you "whistle while you work," you lay the groundwork for the era of vibrational medicine, glimmering in tantalizing promise across the chasm of social transformation. Know that each time you use song and loving touch to ease the suffering of another, you bring the mighty promise of vibrational healing that much closer to your experience.

12

The Warming Earth:
Global Crisis and Restoration

Of all the challenges facing humankind in a parlous era, one holds both the greatest peril and the greatest promise: global warming. In truth, global warming is but one facet of a multi-dimensional ecological crisis whose fearsome potential you are only beginning to recognize. Before addressing the issue itself, let us take a look at the Earth from the perspective of ecological holism.

The Global Fabric

Every planet is an ecological system of greater or lesser complexity. As Nature's fundamental principle is balance, every planet settles into a stable equilibrium, however dynamic its surface may be. Ecological balance is maintained by redundancy and by reserve; that is, systems are set up to weather periods of stress and instability by calling upon redundant, overlapping systems which restore equilibrium. Ecological systems also hold reserves of energy and essential elements which can be called upon when regular stores are strained. The overall design is one of dynamic elasticity which can easily withstand and compensate for stresses and strains, restoring a stable equilibrium.

Earth is an exceptional planet for a number of reasons, including its extraordinarily lively and dynamic surface; its high water content; its equable temperature range; and its mix of atmospheric and telluric elements enabling life to thrive. Unlike other planets, which have little difficulty in maintaining equilibrium, Earth has an exceptionally dynamic and volatile environment, both atmospheric and telluric: from earthquakes to tornadoes, the party never stops. This requires greater stores of redundancy and reserve, and a greater elasticity, to maintain equilibrium. In fact, Earth rarely settles at static equilibrium; its dynamism is its equilibrium. Earth is the "child" of the Universe—impulsive, erratic, energetic, volatile, dynamic—spinning amid "mature," stable planet neighbors. Earth, then, is an exception to the general rule that planets seek a stable equilibrium. Earth seeks—in fact requires—a dynamic volatility to maintain its "equilibrium" of perpetual swirl and upheaval, the requisite of life. Water flows, wind howls, mountains crumble, the crust heaves, the heavens storm—this is Earth's equilibrium.

The Curious Animal

Into this uniquely dynamic and volatile sphere arrived a uniquely intelligent and curious animal, humankind. Unlike all other animals, designed to thrive in distinct ecological niches, humankind is designed to thrive nowhere and everywhere. Naked, plodding, clumsy, deaf and dumb (by animal standards), humanity must survive by wits (and opposable thumbs) alone.

All was well until human wits devised civilization a mere ten millennia ago. Here humankind diverted from the path of Nature and assumed powers of the gods. An unnatural social order—for humankind is meant to live in small tribes—civilization strips away the existential security, the ineffable comfort, that comes from living within Nature's design. It is as if humanity were offered a Faustian bargain—enjoy the greater material comfort and security of civilization at the price of existential *in*security—and eagerly seized the material reward at the expense of its soul.

Existential *in*security is the corollary of civilization. No longer resting in the primordial security of tribe and forest, humanity casts itself out from the Garden, condemned to forever cobble together security and sustenance where they may be found, only to risk having them snatched away. Seeking to ameliorate its insecurity, humanity snatches at trinkets of earthly security—wealth, power, land—but no one—the mighty leader, the moneyed banker, the lord of ranch or manor—can ever rest in easy security. Always the princes are conniving about the throne, the natives restless, the peasants plotting, the barbarians approaching, the economy buckling, the crops failing, the job shaky, the rent rising, the health insurance unaffordable, the government oppressive, the priests self-serving. Small wonder that in colonial America hundreds of colonists fled civilization for the existential security of tribal living.

Existential insecurity is like a constant static in the ears that vexes and clouds the mind, impairing clear thought and true vision. Life is lived on the surface: getting and having and keeping, struggling to forge an island of security amid a sea of insecurity, yet never attaining it; for true security—existential security—is impossible to realize in civilization. You made the pact with the devil: now enjoy its fruit.

With the mind clouded and vexed, with the ego consumed with patching together a fragile security, what hope is there of retaining the wisdom of the ages, born of a deep, instinctive bond with Nature? Who can walk in the footsteps of the shaman padding through his forest home, recognizing the plant healers, the plant nourishers, the plant teachers, partners of humankind? Who can view the spider, the jaguar, the snake, and feel the ineffable, primal bond of Universal Life Force flowing in their veins as in yours? Who can feel the *absolute security* of living cocooned in the natural world, as if the skin dissolves and one's essence melts into the plants and animals, as theirs melts into yours; a boundaryless pulsing ocean of free-flowing *Life*?

The Global Crisis

Yours is an era of globalization, when national boundaries crumble as people, products, and pollution crisscross the globe. So brilliant has humankind been at taming and conquering the wild Earth—bulldozing the natural world in service to human need—that the planet could well be renamed Humanity. A smug complacency would be premature, however, as humanity's triumph is not yet fully realized. Only now—with the advent of scientific instruments capable of measuring the changes, and the further advent of communication technologies linking the globe in borderless networks—are you beginning to glimpse the gravity of the crisis you have created.

For, in the end, yours is not planet Humanity and you cannot plunder it without consequence. As noted above, every ecological system, from a tiny pond to a planet, draws upon redundancies and reserves to weather periods of stress and restore equilibrium. This means that as an ecological system begins to suffer damage, the damage will not be apparent because compensatory mechanisms mask it. There comes a point, however—a tipping point—when redundancies and reserves have been exhausted and the system begins to unravel in a downward spiral of collapse.

Global warming, then, is not a single process, with a single cause, a single consequence, and a single cure. It is the most obvious manifestation of an unraveling global ecology with many causes and many consequences; the blaring siren drawing attention to a planet that has exhausted itself trying to compensate for the predations of humankind. It is also not the most dire potential outcome of an unraveling ecology; it is a precursor of worse to come if its lessons are not heeded.

As you understand it, global warming is a steady rise in temperature, propelled by excess atmospheric carbon, which threatens a number of catastrophic results. As temperatures rise, plant and animal species unable to adapt to rapid change face extinction. A rising sea temperature threatens disruption of oceanic circulatory patterns, and calamitous loss of species. Storms become more severe and frequent. As glacial ice—the planet's water reserves—melts, sea levels rise, threatening coastal cities. The loss of ice cover—which deflects the sun's rays—threatens further glacial melting, in a perverse, self-perpetuating cycle of further warming begetting further warming.

Ultimately, even those on high ground, far from the coasts, suffer the effects. Dramatic changes in weather patterns portend reduced rainfall and more drought in agricultural areas, yielding less food to feed more hungry mouths. Massive migrations of the displaced overwhelm national boundaries and social capacities. Wars erupt over food and fresh water supplies. And so on.

As you understand it, global warming is caused by the burning of fossil fuels which pumps excess carbon dioxide into the atmosphere, triggering a greenhouse effect. There are other factors, however, not yet recognized. One is the electrification of the globe. In its natural state, the Earth relies on a clear and unhindered flow of "information" from the heavens to the ground, and back again, in a cycle of mutual awareness. There is no "mind" processing this information; the system operates chemically and energetically: the chemical and energetic composition of wind and rain is absorbed by plants and the ground, "apprising" them of larger patterns encircling the globe. The chemical and energetic emissions from plants and animals, in turn, "apprise" the atmosphere of events and trends down below. Again, it is an unconscious, unmediated system of information exchange that stabilizes and balances the Earth.

As an example, where pressure builds up in the Earth's crust as rock grinds against rock, the growing tension is transmitted vibrationally through the crust and into the atmosphere. When the tension is so great that equilibrium must be restored sharply (otherwise known as an earthquake), this too will be broadcast before the event. It is well known that animals sense these portentous vibrations and seek safety and shelter. The system has a larger purpose than transmitting earthquake warnings, but this is one of the benefits to animate life.

Another example is in the atmosphere, where fierce storms rage. At times tension builds in the clouds and must be released in torrents of rain and jabs of lightning. Lightning is the intense and rapid "grounding" of atmospheric tension, safely dispersed in the Earth. As always, the purpose is balance: balancing the fierce volatility of atmosphere with the sturdy quiescence of bedrock. Believe it or not, the system is set up so that lightning discharges where it will cause the least damage to animate life. No overseeing mind enforces this; it happens naturally, as living bodies, heavy with fluid, are less efficient conductors and transmitters of electrical energy than, say, trees or stone. If the purpose is to ground electrical energy, that purpose is best served by striking a rock or tree.

The electrification of the globe interferes with the energetic information exchange between bedrock and atmosphere. It is a layer of thick static which mangles energetic messages passing through it. Atmosphere and bedrock lose their smooth exchange and communicate in garbled fragments. As well, the ocean floor is lined with electrical and communication cables, so the deep communion from ocean depths to atmosphere is warped and frazzled.

This bears on global warming because the Earth's ability to accurately gauge a threat to its equilibrium—to recognize it and take compensatory measures—is hampered by the loss of energetic communication. In other words, if humankind had burned all the fossil fuels it has but not harnessed electricity, global warming would not have such severe effects, had it occurred at all. As it is, Earth is blinded and deafened, just when it most needs clear perception to overcome a dire threat to its equilibrium.

Thus the crisis is compounded. First, the Earth cannot compensate for the threat of global warming with all the tools in its arsenal, because it cannot accurately judge the nature of the threat. Second, the electrification of the globe holds other ramifications, for the easy communion between bedrock and atmosphere is impaired. Where patterns of wind and rain might formerly have been scattered more widely, and of moderate intensity, now a blinded Earth unleashes fierce storms; as if lashing out in wild anger. The smooth elasticity of Earth's balancing processes hardens into erratic, powerful swings and jolts.

The Cosmic Picture

Any scientist could offer the overview of global warming and its potential effects we have outlined thus far. Let us turn now to the bigger picture—the metaphysical picture—to understand the deeper meaning of the rising ecological crisis.

All earthly life springs from a nonphysical source. Earth is one venue of activity within the "camouflage" physical system.* Consciousness is the thread binding earthly and immaterial realms: pure consciousness assumes the guise of earthly life, "forgetting" its true origin and participating in a grand drama of intensely physicalized experience. You forget your origins because you must in order to participate fully. If "suspension of disbelief" is a prerequisite to enjoying a play or movie, "suspension of awareness" is the foundation of earthly experience.

Every element of earthly existence has consciousness of a degree and nature commensurate with its form and purpose. Stone and oak and bacteria have their unique shades of consciousness appropriate to their experience. Human consciousness is unique in its dramatic expansion of awareness beyond its closest mammalian cousins. Humans can ponder the meaning of life, communicate their thoughts in sophisticated written and spoken language, and pool resources to forge great civilizations.

---

*See Chapter 8.

Unlike most other beings—animate or otherwise—participating in earthly experience, human souls take care in selecting the time and place of their birth, in order to find just the right mix of birth mother, family, society, culture, historical period, and technological sophistication, that best suits the higher self's purpose for a lifetime. These elements create a crucible of life, imbuing experience with their unique accents, though the grand themes of life—love, power, romance, family, happiness—are eternal regardless of historical background. It is like poring through the great dramas of history, from Sophocles to Shakespeare to Chekov, and choosing the one most compatible with your taste. The grand themes endure; the scenery changes.

All this by way of saying that if an age of unprecedented ecological threat appears overwhelming, and you long to scamper back to a cozy eighteenth-century cottage, realize that you are here now because "you"—meaning your higher self—chose to be here now. If you are middle-aged or older, it is quite possible that the potentials of global warming were not even recognized by souls seeking incarnation in your birth year—that is, whatever cultural and familial elements attracted your soul, "ecological holocaust" was likely not one of them. If you are young, chances are those potentials were crystallizing toward expression and therefore formed part of the "package" of likely life experience.

As mentioned, the grand themes of life—most of which arise in personal and familial relationships—remain eternal regardless of cultural circumstance. Love is the grandest theme of all, and its yearnings and passions and heartbreaks and triumphs are the most powerful experiences in most people's lives, the most deeply enriching (or traumatic) memory traces you carry with you when releasing earthly life. What matters the job, the neighborhood, the weather, the politicians, against the power of love?

The struggle against adversity is another powerful theme, and one higher selves love to employ in fashioning lives of especial intensity; for what greater triumph can a human being know but decades of struggle finally yielding success and approbation; or— equally valid from the higher self's perspective—crushing defeat?

The point is that when you exhale your last breath and release earthly life, you carry with you into the realm of spirit the memory traces of a lifetime. The most significant traces will likely be born of the grand themes of life—triumphs and defeats in love and adversity—while the backdrop of life—cultural, political, historical, ecological—fades to insignificance. This includes global warming, however dramatic its effects may be.

The Rise and Fall of Civilization

There is a larger issue which no one—no scientist or politician—has even realized, yet alone addressed: it is civilization itself that is driving ecological holocaust. Global warming is only the most recent—and most threatening—symptom of a larger global malaise. From deforestation to burning rainforests to strip mining to plundered seas, the planet has been assaulted by civilized societies since the Sumerians first gathered round their king.

It may seem paradoxical, as civilization is more efficient at food production than hunting-and-gathering, but the foundation of civilization is existential insecurity. That insecurity must be assuaged with trinkets of false security—land, money, power, fame—driving civilized persons to forever seek more and better trinkets of security. Worse, the shift from tribal to civilized living means the sundering of the central bonds of tribal life: the deep interpersonal bonds with other members of the tribe; and the instinctive bond with Nature. In their place rises an alienation from others—for who can know and care for millions of strangers?—and an alienation from Nature—which, since the Garden of Eden, has been viewed as a swamp of wickedness, to be held in dominion by humankind.

The irony is that nothing can ever assuage existential insecurity—nothing is ever "enough"—because no trinket can heal the problem at its source: by definition, civilized societies rest on existential insecurity. No matter how much wealth, power, or fame one attains, it is never enough: the insecurity burns and rankles; and everyone hungers after more. Civilization by its very nature—its insecure nature—develops a ruling class, a wealthy class, which lives far beyond the simple satisfaction of human needs, driving the relentless consumption of the Earth. Meanwhile, the Great Unwashed—the masses of the poor, serfs, slaves, and servants who do the hard work of maintaining civilization—live in genuine insecurity, with hunger, poverty, and abuse their miserable lot.

Civilized societies may have had a minor impact on the planet for most of their history, but from the Industrial Age onward, the foundation of modern economics has been the ever more efficient grinding up of "natural resources"—as if the Earth were a supply cabinet forever stocked by indulgent gods. Every modern economy—and those aspiring to that status—rests on this foundation of ecological destruction in the service of economic progress. Liberal or conservative, it matters not: all politicians see a robust economy as the greatest good. But a robust economy, by definition, means the consumption of "natural resources" beyond all need or reason.

Ultimately, then, global warming is not the problem; global warming is a symptom of a larger problem: civilization itself. By definition, civilization induces existential insecurity. By definition, everyone strives to assuage existential insecurity by acquiring security trinkets—land, money, power—whose acquisition means ecological harm. By definition, civilization creates ruling and wealthy classes whose ostentatious displays of trinkets drive even further destruction. Post-Industrial Age, the entire planet is plundered and stripped with murderous rapacity.

We pass no judgment; we do not argue the merits of civilized living versus tribal living. Our point is to underscore that civilization itself—not the burning of fossil fuels—is the larger culprit in a systemic ecological crisis of which global warming is but the most portentous omen. The question facing you, then, is not whether you can weather the effects of global warming—as profound as they will be—but whether this will inspire a deeper examination of the organization and values of civilized society. Like any indulgent parent, the Earth offers plenty of precautionary warnings and cautions before striking—but if those warnings are not heeded, civilization itself may be imperiled.

By its very nature, civilization passes through cycles of birth, growth, maturity, decay, and collapse. A social order founded on existential insecurity cannot endure forever; threats from within and without eventually hobble and destroy it. As long as a civilization is in the ascendant, its citizens can satisfy their ambitions from the growing wealth and power; social cohesion is strong. Once the apex of power, wealth, and prestige is passed—and the first symptoms of decay appear—insecurity intensifies and everyone claws more furiously for a larger share of a shrinking pie. An internally weakened society is easy prey for the barbarians at the gate.

All this is understood to historians and schoolchildren alike—who snicker and shake their heads at the folly of Roman and Aztec leaders—but few recognize that they too rest on a societal foundation as unstable as that underlying Rome or Tenochtitlán. Just as radical changes in temperature and weather patterns threaten mass extinction of plants and animals, so too are the threats to social cohesion—which exacerbate the "decline and fall" phase—intensified in breadth, magnitude, and rapidity. *Civilization as presently constituted cannot stand; the Earth cannot support it.* The threat is that it won't be one civilization falling while others rise from its ashes; the threat is of a worldwide collapse of social order—of civilization itself.

And where will that lead you? Back to your true human selves—your tribal selves, living in harmony with Nature. What form that will take—whether in a smaller-scale, less destructive form of civilization, or a return to pure tribal living—remains to be seen. But whether the agent is global warming, a viral pandemic, or merely an economic depression, the end will be the same: a restoration of humankind's proper place in the natural order.

A Zone of Safety

What is the foundation of civilization, any civilization? Agriculture: settled food production. Agriculture is more efficient than hunting-and-gathering, freeing some members of society to pursue other paths as priests, soldiers, and merchants. Someone has to organize and control the growing complexity, giving rise to a ruling class and monarchy. However vast and high-tech your societies are today, and however remote they appear from the first rude rice plots, they still rest on the efficient and reliable production of food. Imperil that and civilization itself is imperiled.

We mention this because imperiled food production is one of the forecasted effects of global warming. Just as the Earth is groaning under burgeoning billions of hungry human mouths, the ability to feed those mouths will be hindered by erratic weather and temperature patterns. Wars will be fought over increasingly scarce food and fresh water.

This scenario may inspire thoughts of fashioning a personal zone of safety to ride out the global warming crisis, and other crises coincident with or successive to it. Certainly, living in an inner-city apartment, wholly dependent on external systems of utilities, food, and water, risks a helpless impotence should disaster strike. It is not our intent to utter dire prophecies of "the end is near," but we would be remiss if we didn't underscore the risks to civilized life that global warming and other crises portend, and how quickly civilization can unravel.

The great cultural upheaval of the sixties, which shattered the complacent inertia of a society too long riding in ancient ruts, triggered a number of movements of widely disparate themes. It is as if an entire society passed through adolescence, the age when spiritual currents flow most strongly through the psyche. Those currents carry portents of the future, urging a youth (or a society) back on track toward a life aligned with spiritual purpose. Among the many movements were those urging return to a rural lifestyle and tribal living. The "back to the land" movement, the rise of intentional communities, the interest in Native American and Eastern cultures and spirituality—these represent the magnetic attraction of lifestyles lived in harmony with Nature and Spirit; a rejection of the industrial-military-political machinery of alienation, oppression, warfare, and ecocide.

Decades hence, you can recognize those movements as the vanguards of a Great Restoration—we are applying a label to an age that has not yet materialized—in which humankind restores itself to its proper place in the natural order and again lives in harmony with natural and spiritual principles. Millions of people find themselves attracted to these principles; even if they can do no more, at this point, than to send a check to an environmental organization or spiritual movement. Others make a more life-affirming choice to turn away from the machinery of modern civilization and embrace a natural lifestyle, whether motivated as survivalists, communitarians, mystics, or agriculturalists; these are the vanguards of the Great Restoration.

The vanguards will be in a better position—in a Zone of Safety—than those trapped in an unraveling society. Our purpose here is to outline which regions of the planet will be most conducive to establishing a Zone of Safety.

[Note!—and note it well!—our purpose is not to incite fear and anxiety. Our point is to highlight the likely events unfolding in the future as global warming and other crises grip the planet; their effects on civilized societies, particularly food production; and that those already ensconced in a Zone of Safety are likely to weather those crises more securely. From a metaphysical perspective, your higher self is indifferent to the cultural backdrop of your life; it is your emotional life—whose themes are eternal—that matters. From a personal perspective, a return to natural and spiritual living should be motivated by a genuine desire for such a lifestyle, not by fear.]

That said, some areas of the planet are more conducive than others to building a Zone of Safety—and within every country, some areas are better than others. As mentioned, the worst place to be is in an inner-city apartment totally dependent on external systems of light, heat, water, and food. All it takes is a major storm knocking out power for a day—or a riot—to underscore the fragility and vulnerability of such a lifestyle. First, you must have some land to grow food; even a suburban backyard offers such a plot. Second, you need to self-generate electricity and hot water—or decide whether you can live without them at all. Of course, solar-power and hot-water systems require technological expertise to manufacture and install, which may become unavailable during a severe social unraveling—which is why the foresightful install such systems *now*.

The first order of business is to find an area to live in—if not a country to live in. Surprisingly, some First World countries will be among the worst to weather the shock; whereas some Third World countries will offer a smoother ride. There is a mix of factors to consider: geography, altitude, urban/rural, water source, population density, cultural values.

Geography: Generally, areas within 30 to 40 degrees of the equator, north and south, offer the safest haven. Much of the world's population lives within this zone already. Remember that Nature always seeks balance, and that balance is easiest to maintain in regions that don't see severe seasonal shifts over an annual cycle. Regions outside this zone—including northern Europe, the northern United States, and Canada—by the very nature of their profound seasonal variations, are more fragile and vulnerable to extremes, including more severe winters and storms. Life is simply more difficult to sustain in already adverse climates likely to become more so.

Everywhere in the world, coastal areas are to be avoided. Rising sea levels threaten cities, groundwater, and coastal agriculture; hotter temperatures portend unbearably torrid weather; collapsing fisheries threaten loss of food and livelihoods; more severe hurricanes, typhoons, and storms will lash the coasts. The spread of tropical, mosquito-borne diseases beyond their traditional zone portends misery and disease. The Zone of Safety begins about 100 miles inland from the coast.

Altitude: Temperature rises as altitude falls. It is best to avoid low-lying areas, including inland areas at or near sea level, because there rising temperatures will be most severe; marginal lands will decline to desert. Climbing in altitude offers a buffer: stable agriculture, an equable climate, fewer storms, fewer mosquitoes. From about 3,000 feet to 10,000 feet at the extremes—and, best, 5,000 to 8,000 feet—is the best altitudinal niche for a Zone of Safety.

Urban/Rural: We have already mentioned that city dwellers are in an especially vulnerable position in the event of disrupted utilities or food supply. Consider, also, the multiplier effect when millions of people are hungry and desperate. Rural areas, or smaller cities and towns surrounded by rural land, are the Zone of Safety.

Water Source: Where does a region's water come from? Rain, glacial melt, rivers, groundwater, a mix? Those regions of the world heavily dependent on glacial runoff for drinking water—Southeast Asia, parts of South America—will suffer drastically as glaciers evaporate. Water is essential to life, and further essential to agriculture. Areas dependent on rainwater may experience dramatic shifts in traditional rainfall patterns; yet these areas are safer than glacier-dependent areas. With improved systems in capturing and storing rainfall—rather than depending on a traditional rainfall cycle—these areas will adapt. Groundwater pumping as a reserve backup—not as a primary source—would enhance safety.

Population Density: Those areas of the world already groaning under burgeoning numbers—Southeast Asia (again); Africa; the cities of the Americas and Europe—are more vulnerable to climate change because they have so many mouths to feed; and their vast numbers breed an alienation which makes social cohesion unravel that much more readily. Again, we look to rural areas, or small cities and towns, to locate a Zone of Safety.

Cultural Values: Cultures differ in their attitude toward outsiders. This is especially relevant if you look outside your home country for a Zone of Safety. If you buy land in a Third World country, can you be sure the laws guarantee your ownership? Will the locals resent or welcome new arrivals? If push comes to shove—and an area suffers severe effects of climate change—will your property and life be respected? Most likely this is dependent on your attitude toward your new neighbors, whether you seek to learn their culture and language and work to integrate yourself into their society; but consider also the cultural mores regarding outsiders—friends or foreigners?

Considering all these factors, those areas that meet all our criteria are inland regions of temperate climate and moderate altitude; namely, the southern United States, Mexico, northern South America, and southern Europe. There are pockets elsewhere—there are pockets everywhere—but Africa is best avoided, as are Southeast Asia and Central America. Islands are to be avoided. There are pockets in the belt stretching from Southeastern Europe through the Caucasus and Kazakhstan, but cultural and linguistics differences, as well as political instability, are to be considered.

Fearlessly Facing the Future

If you find yourself reacting with fear and urgency to this material, such is not our intent. Let us affirm the following:

1. Nothing is written in stone vis-à-vis the effects of global warming and other potential crises. Scientists can model all they like—and their prognostications are of value—but ultimately no one can predict the course of global events; too many variables are involved.

2. Do we predict the collapse of civilization? No, we point out that *in its current manifestation* it is unsustainable: Nature can't replace "natural resources" as fast as they are extracted, ground up, and burned. You can't fuel your cars with dead dinosaurs forever; there are no more dinosaurs to liquefy. How, whether, to what degree civilization will decline is as unknowable as the state of the planet a century hence; for your infinitely clever species may well avoid the worst with technology not yet conceived. Still, the trend must be

toward restoring a lifestyle more in harmony with natural and spiritual principles.

3. Remember that you chose to be here in this time of turmoil and transformation—"you" meaning your higher self—and that you are meant to participate meaningfully in the family and culture in which you were born. Working together to avoid the worst potentials of global warming is a greater triumph than retreating to a survivalist bunker, gun in hand. Further, the mass migrations likely to occur—and the smaller-scale relocation of North Americans and Europeans to congenial climes—promises a mixing of previously discrete racial, ethnic and cultural groups, leading toward a blended human family: progenitors of the Great Restoration.

4. If you still feel fear or anxiety about the coming period of upheaval, reframe the issue. Can civilization as currently constituted continue its rapacious destruction of the Earth? Do you want it to? Can humankind expand its numbers ad infinitum, until every other species is crowded off the planet? Do you want it to? Do you approve of restoring a smaller-scale human lifestyle in harmony with natural and spiritual principles? Viewed this way, the long-term effects of the global warming crisis are salutary: reducing human impact on the planet; restoring a sustainable human population living an ecologically harmonious lifestyle.

The fundamental law of Nature is balance. Crises, by definition, are extraordinary events, erupting only because a system has spun far out of equilibrium and can return to balance only with severe corrective measures. Once the crisis has passed, and equilibrium is restored, the system is stronger for having weathered the crisis. This holds for both the planet and your civilization.

Crises are never pretty, and the ensuing century portends much upheaval, calamity, and suffering. Such is the ineluctable consequence of humankind's pursuit of technological mastery while neglecting its spirituality. Technology and spirituality are meant to progress in tandem, the latter tempering the former. The Great Restoration means just that: restoring a certain humility to humankind—no longer self-appointed masters of the planet, but one species among many, living in respectful harmony with the Earth and its creatures, resting on sturdy pillars of science and spirit.

In the end, the Zone of Safety lies inside you: for the one who walks in inner peace and harmony meets any crisis with deep equanimity. May you walk in peace.

13

Rage and Madness:
The Roots of Terrorism

One of your era's most frightening and infuriating phenomena is terrorism. Not only the United States, but also European countries—and even Islamic states—are targets of militant Islamic hatred toward the West. Many elements are intertwined in this complex global phenomenon, which we will tease apart and examine with an eye toward a deeper understanding.

First, a definition: terrorism is the individual's usurpation of war-making powers reserved to national governments. For all its apparently uncontrolled nature, modern warfare is as regulated by international agreements as are commerce or aviation. That is, states agree on the rules governing the conduct of war, and what acts are permissible or not on the battlefield and in the treatment of prisoners of war. Generally, reckless attacks on civilians are forbidden. Also, of course, national governments arrogate to themselves the exclusive right to wage war on other states.

Terrorism violates these international protocols root and branch. First, nongovernmental agents—individuals or groups—assume the powers of warfare reserved to national governments. Second, instead of attacking military personnel, civilians are deliberately targeted to enhance shock value and incite widespread panic. Confidence in government—which failed to detect and deter the attack—is shaken. National governments are thus doubly outraged—first by an act of war by an "unauthorized" agent, and then by their citizens' anger and doubt directed toward them.

Terrorism has a long history, for nations are forever under attack from without and within. Many nations, in their official histories, revere the terrorist acts of their forebears which led to the downfall of oppressive governments. The Boston Tea Party, the storming of the Bastille, the revolutionary movements of North and South American colonies against their European masters—all were terrorist acts at the time, regarded by the threatened powers with the same revulsion with which you now regard suicide bombers and airplanes rammed into skyscrapers. Context and time determine whether terrorist acts are reviled or revered by history.

The Tragedy of Civilization

In the essay on Global Warming we discussed the existential insecurity that underlies civilized societies. Let us review and further explore this.

Imagine being born a Navajo, a Quechua, a Zulu, an Aborigine, in the long sweep of time before the age of European exploration and conquest. You are born into a people with an identity stretching back to the distant origins of time, beyond all trace of memory. Your tribal identity is fundamental to your being, permeating your cells and psyche. Your family wraps you in even deeper blond-bonds as the progeny of an unbroken stream of living blood flowing back to the primordial Man and Woman. You live embedded in sacred Nature; your people know every secret of the plants, animals, seasons, and cosmos, calling them by familial name, weaving them in mythic stories binding you tighter in tribal identity and meaning. The shamans of your people know Life and the Cosmos yet deeper than this, communing with the plant-spirits, the animal-spirits, and the gods; performing rituals to appease and implore the wild forces swirling about you. You live in a nested cocoon of meaning—first, tribal identity; second, familial blond bonds; third, Nature; fourth, Cosmos; fifth, Spirit.

This is existential security; *this* is the ineffable security of knowing who you are and where you belong—you, your people, the natural world, the spirit realm—the security of an irrefrangible personal and tribal identity that can never be shattered or lost.

Tribes develop no law codes, no police, no courts, no jails, and no government. Yes, tribal elders guide their people; but those elders mature naturally into their authority, after a lifetime of demonstrated wisdom. Their decisions benefit all members of the tribe; thus their authority is unquestioned. Tribes are communitarian in the sharing of food and resources.

Tribes are perpetually self-regenerating; they suffer no "decline and fall" period of decay. What is natural endures as unconsciously as the flow of seasons or path of the sun.

Central to tribal perpetuity and freedom from government is managed numbers. There is a limit to the number of individuals who can share a tribe and maintain tribal cohesion.* Tribes below this threshold easily maintain the networks of family and affiliation crucial to tribal cohesion: everyone knows everyone else—their name, family, history, and place in the tribe. A tribe growing beyond the natural threshold must split or risk disintegration: for where numbers grow too large, alienation, hierarchy, and power relationships arise.

These are the features of tribal living—a deeply rooted tribal identity; family bonds; cultural mythos; communion with Nature; managed numbers. It is almost impossible to describe—or for you to imagine—the profound, ineffable *security* underlying tribal living. Tribal history, ancestral blood, myth and meaning, wild Nature—imagine the *certainty*, the *solidity* of identity in such a milieu.

Our aim is not to romanticize tribal living nor to gloss over its uglier aspects. Clearly, more than one tribe starved to death in all its ineffable security; and savagery that would shock the modern conscience was often the norm. Our point is to underscore that tribal living is the natural form of human social organization—the one that evolved with the species over countless millennia—and that, naturally, this is the social order to which human beings are best suited; the best "fit" for the human psyche.

Civilization is a recent upstart. It arose when a few clever individuals discovered that cultivating wild grains yielded more consistent and bountiful harvests, with less effort than hunting and gathering. Settled agriculture meant releasing the nomadic lifestyle of tribalism. It is still possible for agricultural tribes to maintain tribal identity and cohesion as long as their numbers are managed. But as numbers grow beyond the threshold of tribal cohesion, and settled tribes become settled villages, some organization is required to manage the burgeoning complexity and numbers. On a very small scale, this was the template of civilization: a governing class, wielding power and authority; and a larger working class taking

---

* British anthropologist Rodney Dunbar sets the limit of tribal cohesion at about 150 individuals.

orders. From this primal template has grown the massive complexity of civilization, with its kings and priests and warriors and slaves.

The tragedy of civilization is twofold. One is its loss of the existential security of tribal living, stripped away by living among countless strangers—of differing bloodlines, cultures, and religions—leaving a howling wound in the psyche: existential *in*security. Because civilization is unnatural, nothing about it is perpetually self-regenerating: civilized societies decline and fall with clockwork regularity; leaders win and lose power by ballot or bullet; nations are swallowed by larger nations; economies buckle and heave; new gods arise and are forgotten; jobs, houses, and fortunes are won and lost; the very foundation of life is a gnawing, unquenchable insecurity. Appease it as you might with trinkets of security—power, wealth, land, fame—you can never quench that insecurity; it forever festers and burns.

The second tragedy of civilization is the sheer magnitude of suffering its produces. The ruling class—as insecure as the lowest slave—forever seeking to aggrandize its wealth and power, finds this easiest with a stable of slaves; or, in modern, more "enlightened" times, the working poor. Earning and eating just enough to keep body and soul together, this vast underclass generates the wealth only their superiors enjoy. Nations are forever warring in hope of gaining more land, more resources, more wealth, more power; inflicting incalculable suffering and death on, again, the underclass of soldiers. Millions go hungry while the elite feast. The communitarian ethos of the tribe is shattered by the vertical hierarchy of civilization; religious, social, and evolutionary doctrines are pressed into service to rationalize the inequity and assuage the rudimentary conscience of the ruling class.

Stop for a moment and simply ponder the sheer breadth of suffering now occurring about the globe. Think of the nations at war; the areas of widespread hunger, disease, and misery; the vast swarms of the underclass scratching out a living at the margins of society; the poisonous religious dogmas; the racist, sexist, classist, homophobic traditions barring most of the Earth's people from realizing their potential. Beyond human suffering, of course, lies a more immense suffering—of the plant and animal species trampled and exterminated in humankind's relentless consumption of the planet. You really can't take it all in—this enormous planetary suffering—both because your mind can't conceive it all, and because you are numb. Going numb is a prerequisite to civilized living: shutting out the outrage of the conscience at the grotesque inequalities and affronts to human dignity that are the essence of civilization. Numbed, insensate, riddled with insecurity: this is the state of the civilized person.

If we sound like a ranting Marxist, such is not our intent. But because you are numb, strong words must be used to break through your deadened apathy and your instinctive defense of the benefits of civilization. We don't argue those benefits, but point out the massive suffering that underlies them. Even the well-fed denizens of the West suffer from intrusive, overweening government; an unstable, increasingly multinational economy; diseases linked to lifestyle and diet; stale, dogmatic religion; an overcrowded, degraded world. Everyone suffers in civilization, the difference being in degree.

The Ultimate Security Trinket

The security trinkets we have mentioned—land, power, wealth, fame—are traditionally the sole province of the ruling classes. In modern times, in progressive states, a comfortable middle class enjoys its share as well. But what of the poor—bereft of land, power, and wealth—even of control over their own persons—what security trinket have they to ameliorate their misery?

Marx said religion is the opiate of the poor. We might add that religion is the security trinket of the poor. Without hope of earthly power or wealth, they can only look above and beyond: into heaven, or a future life; and there place their hopes and dreams for a small measure of security and comfort. The world's great religions rest—like the rest of civilization—on the backs of the poor, who are their most devoted followers.

While religion is the only security trinket available to the poor, its appeal is universal; every religion counts devout believers among all social classes. Who *wouldn't* want divine favor and blessings on life, family, and nation? Who *wouldn't* want to be singled out by God or gods for favorable treatment? What leader *wouldn't* want priestly blessing on wars and conquests? Religion is free—anyone can pray—and, with its tantalizing promise of divine favor and eternal bliss, deeply appealing to the perpetually insecure members of civilized societies.

The Age of Jihad

We mentioned that national leaders often seek religious blessing on their worldly affairs, seeking to justify them to their people by invoking the deity (an easy sell, the people being just as eager for divine favor). No army marches off to war without the requisite blessing by priest/rabbi/imam. Yet, returning to religion's universality, anyone can similarly invoke religious justification for any act, however heinous or violative of religious principle.

A study of the crackpots of history, who arrogated to themselves the personal mission of reforming the world according to their private ideals, would reveal that many were strongly religious—in their own perverse way—and felt called by God to wreak vengeance on a sinful world. It is important to view this psychological mechanism for what it is—madness wrapped in a self-rationalizing religious veneer. No ego can say to itself, "I'm an angry lunatic acting out of gross madness." Instead, the ego seeks justification by invoking the deity. "Being on a personal mission from God" trumps "gross madness" as a justifying motive. In other cases, a homegrown terrorist may wrap himself in the flag of patriotism; again, "avenging patriot" trumps "disgruntled loser" as ego-soothing motive.

As an aside, in your age many otherwise sophisticated persons view the murderous deeds of "religious" leaders and terrorists, and blame religion for a world enmeshed in lethal chaos. No religious text—save perhaps the Torah—glorifies and encourages wanton warfare and the slaughter of innocents. A sophisticated person sees through the religious justification to the real motive—base lust for power, or barking madness—and there lays the blame.

Islamic terrorism is an oxymoron. Nothing in the Koran justifies the deliberate and wanton murder of innocents, nothing. While the Koran doesn't share Christ's message of "turning the other cheek"—a value no "Christian" nation has ever followed—it urges restraint in warfare and equable relations with other faiths. As terrorism fails the test of any religious justification, we must look elsewhere for the real motive behind so-called "Islamic" terrorism.

History, ancient and modern, offers a clue. During its Golden Age stretching over five or six centuries, Islamic civilization was the crown jewel of the world, whose influence continues to reverberate in your age. Arcing from Asia to Europe, this polycultural empire is renowned for its achievements in science, the arts, scholarship, and ethics: tolerant, humanistic, and rational in pursuit of scientific truth (within limits of the time).

Fast-forward to today. Despite its global prominence due to the chance wealth of oil beneath its sands, the Muslim world not only doesn't hold the world's respect, it is held in revulsion by many for its archaic and primitive culture. Veiled women, hands lopped off in public, strict moral codes, stifled intellect and curiosity—these are the features of conservative Muslim cultures. Who in the post-Enlightenment West would regard them with anything but repugnance?

Give the Muslim world credit, however, for remaining true to its religious text and following its admonishments literally. The veiling of women, the death penalty for various offenses, the chopping off of robbers' hands—these are penalties prescribed in the Koran which are dutifully carried out by traditional Muslims. In the Western world, adherents of Judeo-Christian religions employ a selective adherence to scriptural edicts, for the Old Testament (Torah) sets out a number of offenses for which the punishment is death. It has been some time since a child was stoned to death for speaking rudely to his parents.

So in the modern age, power, prestige, and wealth lie with the West—Europe and North America—to the burning resentment of Muslims, who recall with anguish the glory days of their empire. The thirst for revenge, for global power and respect, burns hot in the hearts of those who once knew power and glory and, despite their oil wealth, are regarded with repugnance by those ruling the world.

Ultimately, terrorism is born of impotence. It is a furious lashing out of those bereft of power and influence, striking out against those they view as depriving them of their due. The suicide bomber strapping explosives to his chest and destroying himself and bystanders is deluding himself if he thinks his death means anything but the ultimate self-abnegation of the impotent. His act violates the Koran; the slaughter of innocents offends Allah; he only strengthens the state he despises.

Again: terrorism is an act of private madness or revenge; it can never be justified by religion. As with any madness, religion is often invoked as justification, to assuage the ego and elevate an act of impotent revenge to holy war. Intelligent persons should see through the delusional self-justification and recognize the act for what it is.

The challenge of your age is that globalization, mass movement of peoples, and ever more refined killing technologies make it that much easier for terrorists to inflict spectacular damage on target nations. This gets them the media attention they crave—at last, elevation to world importance!—thus winning a hollow victory. Hollow because the West will never be taken down by sporadic acts of terrorism, but only strengthened by such attacks.

Agents of Disequilibrium

We have mentioned (ad nauseum!) that the foundational principle of Nature is balance. Every natural system, from atoms to galaxies, strives to maintain a stable equilibrium. But there is a difference between equilibrium and stasis: equilibrium is life, stasis is death. There must always be an elasticity, an allowance for movement and change, the adaptability to meet and master fresh challenges: what constitutes equilibrium in one moment differs from successive equilibria. A natural system is forever in motion, forever adapting and self-modifying, forever forging new states of equilibrium. Equilibrium is dynamism held within sustainable bounds.

Nature thus "packages" agents of disequilibrium within every natural system. Their purpose is to disrupt equilibrium, to prevent deadly stasis, and to force the system to adapt or die. The wind is a universal agent of disequilibrium—it challenges trees, plants, and animals to withstand its force. Dead and diseased trees, unable to resist, topple. Only the strong, the resilient, the adaptable survive, strengthened for the challenge. Fire is another agent of disequilibrium, and while its incendiary power vaporizes many smaller life forms, larger, stronger trees not only survive but thrive in the newly cleared forest. Wind, fire, rain, the shifting seasons: all are agents of disequilibrium forcing natural systems to adapt or die.

You carry many such agents in your body—bacteria and viruses that could turn deadly under the right conditions. Even your immune system can turn against you. A healthy body keeps these agents of disequilibrium in check, beating back their thrusts and parries, restoring an ever-shifting equilibrium, stronger for the challenge.

We raise this seemingly digressive material because it carries over into human society. Every human society—be it a tribe in the jungle or an industrial state—is governed by natural principles.

Within and without, agents of disequilibrium are forever at work. Criminals are such agents, disrupting the "equilibrium" of safe streets. A riot is an explosive agent of disequilibrium, with the state losing control to the mob, followed by an equilibrium of heightened state power. The economy is prey to countless agents of disequilibrium, as any investor knows, forever shifting in its mercurial temper. A marriage suffers constant agents of disequilibrium tearing at the marital bond, testing its strength and resilience.

Terrorism is an agent of disequilibrium. It challenges the equilibrium of the state's control over its borders and its protection of citizens' lives and property. It challenges the equilibrium of personal freedom versus state control. It challenges the equilibrium of a global empire with military bases planted in the land of the Koran. It challenges the equilibrium of a smug complacency in national power and rightness of course.

Terrorism forces awareness and consideration of issues which might otherwise remain buried. Should perfect security be purchased at the price of lost civil liberties? Are constitutional protections still valid in an age of global travel and weapons of mass lethality? Can Islam be integrated into the West or is it alien and indigestible? Should there be a global empire with military bases girdling the globe, including the Middle East? These are questions only modern peoples even need to consider, but they all point back to that primordial principle of equilibrium being disrupted by agents designed for the purpose.

Terrorism is nothing new, then: there have always been self-righteous zealots seeking to reform the world according to their personal visions. Most such crackpots were humored or dismissed in their age and few did much damage. What differs in your age is that, first, agents of disequilibrium may act from half a world away; second, the lethality of their attacks is aggravated by modern technology; third, by wrapping themselves in the flag of Muslim vengeance, they elevate their personal pathology to jihad, holy war— and many in the West take the bait.

Being attacked by foreigners—especially bearded, turbaned foreigners living in caves—evokes a fury and thirst for revenge that homegrown terrorists can't inspire. What is lost in all the rage and retaliatory warfare is a deeper, more subtle analysis of the circumstances triggering the terrorist attacks, and a discussion among citizens of the global empire as to the costs and morality of maintaining that empire. From such an analysis and discussion might emerge a new equilibrium—a new balance point of heightened perception and conscious awareness of the empire's reach, motives, and conduct.

As it is, the crudity of the response, from political leaders and citizens alike, is an opportunity lost—and a dangerous sign. For when a system doesn't perceive agents of disequilibrium clearly, and respond with appropriate adaptive measures, the system is weakened. Refusing to acknowledge or discuss the issues that people of a global empire ought to be openly debating—instead waging interminable warfare in the heart of the Islamic world, pushing otherwise reasonable people into the arms of the fanatics—can only portend even more severe shocks in the future.

Let us repeat for emphasis: *there is no such thing as a war of religion, or a holy war.* No religious text endorses the slaughter of innocents and children or the barbaric abuse of prisoners of war. War—or its "unofficial" version, terrorism—is always fought either out of personal madness, or base lust for security trinkets of land, power, wealth, and glory. The religious wrapping is an afterthought, an egoic self-rationalization.

You live in a time of significant turmoil. Ecological changes, most prominently global warming, portend severe stresses on the global ecology and human societies. Compounding these stresses are terrorist attacks on Western states, challenging their tradition of open borders and free societies. Recognize all these stresses as agents of disequilibrium—*without which systems grow static and die*—and further recognize that a system that perceives those agents clearly, and adapts appropriately, is stronger for the challenge: forging an enhanced, more resilient equilibrium. Such is true of the atom, the mollusk, the virus, and the elephant—and such is true of you and the society in which you live.

May you meet and adapt to your life's challenges with conscious perception and an ever-more-refined equilibrium!

14

Projection and Polarity:
The Psychology of Politics

You live in an age of polarized politics, with "left" and "right" hunkering down in bunkers of rigid ideology, exchanging potshots while the populace huddles in the middle, dodging shrapnel. Or so it seems, if the image presented by the media is accurate. It isn't: as always, the vast majority of people go about their lives paying scant attention to politics, and the putative polarization is largely a creation of the media and politicians themselves.

That said, yours is an age of increasingly rigid ideology and fear-based chest-beating, but largely on the conservative side of the spectrum. Because it affects both the inner workings of society, and the response to international crises like global warming, in this essay we examine the origin of "left" and "right" political perspectives.

The Age of Fear

Thinking back to your ancient forebears, living in small tribes embedded in wild Nature, there was no such thing as politics per se. Tribes have leaders, but, again, those leaders mature naturally into their authority; they are not elected or deposed. Like everything else in tribal life, the assumption and exercise of authority is organic, innate, instinctive. Politics as you know it, then, is unique to civilized societies.

The fundament of civilized living is the loss of the tribe's existential security, stripped away to leave a howling existential insecurity. "Fear" is a simpler term for existential insecurity: the perpetual fear for one's security amid the chronic instability of civilized society. Everyone is afraid, to a greater or lesser degree, in civilization. The meanest Untouchable fears hunger and abuse; the loftiest emperor fears poison and invasion. No civilized person sleeps untroubled sleep.

Politics—meaning the organization, concentration, and transition of power—is the central feature of civilized societies. Organization—the management of the various realms of activity (commerce, religion, warfare) of a civilized state. Concentration—the relative concentration or diffusion of power. Transition—how power passes from one leader to the next. The various experiments in power organization—dictatorship, democracy, socialism, anarchy, monarchy—reflect the search for the configuration ensuring maximum stability in a society; which, after all, is the first order of business.

In a social order where everyone feels insecure, everyone is driven to assuage that insecurity by obtaining food, land, wealth, or power—or all of them. Left unmanaged, a mad scramble would ensue, resulting in perpetual disorder and bloodletting as gangs and families fight and kill for their share and others': only the strong survive. The only reason you don't live like this is because you acquiesce to the authority of government to provide basic security and stability. The individual willingly surrenders his personal power to the government, in exchange for the relative stability it ensures. Politics deals with the questions: Who wields the power? how much? how long? and how does it pass?

For most of civilization's sweep, the power matrix was simple: an emperor stood atop a pyramid, power concentrated in his hands. Call it dictatorship, authoritarianism, fascism, communism—power concentrated at the top and directed downward is the "natural" organization of civilized society. Natural because civilized societies rest on fear and insecurity, which is best assuaged by a firm grip from above. Also, leaders themselves are riddled with fear for their power; and—as with all security trinkets—forever grasp at more, in an ultimately futile quest to quench that gnawing insecurity.

Those living in democracies, and convinced that theirs is the best way of life, might consider those countries experiencing the loss of firm state control. Russians pining for Stalin; Spaniards for Franco; Germans for Hitler—such longing for statism seems inconceivable to free peoples. But *security*, not freedom, is the primal need of civilized peoples; and a leader who keeps the trains running and the larder full is more revered than the hapless prime minister overseeing chaos and want.

The Human Psyche

However obscured it may be by centuries of political philosophizing, the meaning of politics boils down to this: *How shall we assuage our existential insecurity?* How shall we mollify our fear? How shall we forge stability amidst disorder? From the first Sumerian king to today's presidents, the central challenge remains the same: the search for security, for stability. That search is driven by fear, the ubiquitous existential insecurity of civilized peoples.

The political spectrum appears to represent a range of thinking about how best to organize and manage society. In truth, two discrete phenomena are at work; one is that central challenge of civilized society: forging security amidst insecurity. The second phenomenon is the human psyche. Let us digress for a moment to discuss this unique and complex construct.

Evolutionists are hard-pressed to explain how the relatively simple psychology of primates radically effloresced into the complexity of the human psyche. If you are reading this, you are probably open to an alternative explanation: the human psyche originates in the realm of spirit and is "impressed" into individual minds, each with a unique template fashioned from the primal pool of human consciousness. That primal pool—what Jung called the collective unconscious—is the repository of all human psychological potential. It contains everything from Neanderthal primitivism (a remarkably durable strand of consciousness!) to the far reaches of a rarefied spirit-psychology you can't even imagine. Each individual's psyche is carefully crafted by the higher self to align with the age and birthplace of the individual. It limits and defines the range of thought and experience available within that lifetime.

We have mentioned that those individuals born within a given time period carry a common energetic "set point." That set point is a psychic cornerstone binding a generation to shared experience; a boundary delimiting the range of psychological reach. It would serve little purpose to have levitating gurus, Cro-Magnon berry gatherers, and Chaldean occultists lumped into the same village. Binding a generation to a common set point ensures a smooth commonality to society.

The Spectrum of Fear

While the set point is common to a generation, there is a flexible spectrum of potential along which the members of a generation may range. In civilized society, the central task is always the quenching of fear, the search for security. So the political spectrum, as you know it, represents a range of reactions to fear, to forging security amidst insecurity. However obscured that central problem may be beneath the complexities of modern society, it ever suffuses the political conversation.

The entire political spectrum, from "left" to "right," addresses existential fear and insecurity. What do those gradations mean, then? And why would a given individual gravitate toward one pole or the other? Why do most people rest comfortably in the middle? Here is where individualized psychology comes into play.

The human psyche is infinitely complex, and it is not our purpose to dissect it here. Suffice it to say that one of its characteristics is its degree of flexibility, elasticity, when faced with novel challenges. Novel challenges—another term for those agents of disequilibrium forever prowling about, seeking to disrupt deadly stasis. How does a person respond in novel situations, or under great stress or challenge? retreat? fall back on old patterns that worked in the past? or embrace new ideas and behaviors? The psyche's degree of flexibility determines the response.

In general, newborn babies have the most flexible psyches of all; everything is brand new and they eagerly take it all in, eager to adapt. By middle age, flexibility has diminished and one settles into comfortable, familiar patterns. By old age, in most people, flexibility has hardened to psychic sclerosis.

Relative flexibility is one of the characteristics impressed into the psyche when fashioning the unique psychological template for a lifetime. So while everyone travels the same path from birth to death—from super-flexibility to super-rigidity—the degree of inborn flexibility ranges from person to person.

Of course, the psyche is not fashioned by the higher self and impressed into neonatal psychology, to remain fixed throughout life.

A child's birth family—especially the mother—and cultural milieu further shape the psyche. Where discipline is harsh, the child learns fear, insecurity, shame, and resentment toward authority. Where discipline is light and cheerful, and the child guided by love, the child learns trust and openness.

Again, a full discussion of the psychology involved is beyond this essay. Suffice it to say that human psychology is a blend of the primal psychological template fashioned by the higher self, and biographical experience which further shapes and colors the psyche.

The Drama of I

You imagine that you perceive your life and world clearly, that you base your political values on solid principles you can easily explain and defend; and that your desire to see the world operate in line with your values is born of soundness of judgment and clarity of vision. If only the world were run according to *your* ideals, all would be well, right?

You may have heard the expression "You create your own reality." This doesn't mean the universe is your personal creation, or that it isn't real. It means that you *never* perceive reality with perfect clarity; that you *never* base your political values on universal principles; and that you *never* seek to change the world out of compassion or wisdom. To begin with, your senses absorb but a fraction of the vibrational information swirling about you; many animals perceive more than you do. What little energetic information passes through the senses is further filtered and sculpted by the ego and psyche. What finally emerges, after passing through sensory and psychic filters, is a fractionated, self-generated hallucination. This you call reality.

Remember that you live in a camouflage physical system. The basis of such a system is a radically private inner life ensured by the blocking of transpersonal thought transmission. You live, then, in a private cocoon of individualized psychology, experience, and meaning. However much you love others, you can never fully know them, burrow down into their psyches and explore every nook and cranny of their being. You are existentially alone.

Further, you don't so much perceive the outside world as project it from within. With the ego's limited range of perceptual focus, the world's richness and variety must be whittled down to a few slender strands of engagement. You can't take it all in, and you can't interact with it all. You engage with those aspects of your world that resonate with you—that speak to your fears, goals, and values—and ignore the rest. You create your own reality, incoming and outgoing, personal and collective.

Psychological Types

Because you live in a given historical time, and because the issues of your age seem linked to political postures, you imagine that liberals and conservatives are defined by the issues they champion, either pro or con. Let us look at this more deeply.

"Liberal" and "conservative" are permanent psychological types—templates in the pool of human consciousness—which, in every age, assume characteristic positions on social issues. A liberal of two centuries ago, if his values remained unchanged, would be a fulminating reactionary today. A conservative of today, transplanted two centuries back, would be a ranting radical of that age. The psychological types are eternal; the issues they embrace ephemeral.

The central problem of civilization is existential insecurity. The entire political spectrum rests on the fear at the heart of civilized societies. How best to assuage that fear; how best to realize security? The poles of the spectrum represent two distinct responses to fear: retreat or embrace.

Starting on the "progressive" side of the spectrum, the approach is to embrace: by expanding the circle of affiliation (meaning the "proper" members of society) to include the downtrodden and marginalized, and by meeting everyone's basic needs, the society as a whole is strengthened and insecurity is assuaged. A plutocratic disparity between the wealthy elite and the impoverished masses is viewed as destabilizing, as the tension between the classes exacerbates societal insecurity. Feeding, clothing, housing, and educating everyone reduces insecurity and stabilizes society. This is the progressive approach.

The conservative approach is to retreat: by withdrawing behind fortified walls of wealth and weaponry, security is won. The poor are viewed as choosing their lot, by indolence or inertia, and undeserving of public handouts. Security is maintained not by equitable sharing of resources, but by force: a vigorous police force maintains law-and-order, and a robust military helps the world see things our way. Society has a sharply vertical hierarchy of the wealthy and powerful at the top, a small middle class, and a mass of Great Unwashed. This is the conservative approach.

The situation becomes more complex. From a *societal* perspective, the conservative approach is more natural. It is natural, when faced with insecurity, to hunker down in a rigid, top-down hierarchy with those at the top barking orders and everyone else bowing and scraping. This is the most natural and efficient way to ensure social stability—it works, as history shows.

But from a *psychological* perspective, the progressive philosophy is more natural. It is natural—because you are tribal creatures and tribes are equitable and communitarian—to wish that all be fed, clothed, housed, and educated. It is natural to expand the circle of affiliation to embrace all members of the human family. It is natural to feel communion with Nature and preserve and protect her wild exuberance. It is natural to be open-minded, tolerant, and curious about new ideas.

On a personal level, the conservative approach is unnatural. If tribal communitarianism is natural, then a wealthy elite dancing on the backs of the poor is unnatural. If expanding the circle of affiliation to embrace the marginalized is natural, then resisting that expansion, pulling the circle's boundary inward, is unnatural. Further, what is life, what is Nature, but ceaseless flux and change and dynamism? To dig in one's heels, to seek regression to a fantasized Golden Age, to stand athwart history yelling "Stop!" is a rejection of Nature, of life itself. And indeed, as we will see, conservatives are Death's handmaidens.

Thus your conundrum. The poles of the political spectrum rest on natural and unnatural elements. On the psychological:societal matrix, conservatives are unnatural:natural and progressives are natural:unnatural. Perhaps this is why neither side, when in power, produces universally satisfactory results. It is an insoluble conundrum for it arises from civilization's being an unnatural social order. Any attempt at social organization, conservative or progressive, will have inefficiencies, repressions, unfairness, disparity, instability, and will ultimately fail: for what is unnatural cannot endure.

The great mass of any society rests in the proverbial "middle of the road," considering the views of left and right but hewing strongly to neither side. Most civilized societies oscillate between left and right sides of the spectrum—bouncing back and forth like tennis balls—as they seek that golden point of perfect security, prosperity, and happiness. It is the Holy Grail of civilized societies—and it can never be found.

Psychological Projections

As mentioned, you don't so much perceive external reality as project your internal self outward onto the world, painting it in personal colors. The world becomes a symbolic stage on which you play out the themes originating from within. Where you fall on the political spectrum—your "resonance" with a certain balance of progressive and conservative elements—reflects the state of your psyche. This process becomes most apparent at the polar extremes of the spectrum—ranting revolutionaries and barking fascists—but holds true for everyone. *First*, you develop a personal psychology; *second*, you embrace a political philosophy aligned with your personal psychology. Political views are secondary, personal psychology primary.

Conservatives and progressives are driven by the same fear: existential insecurity. From a psychological perspective, the progresssive approach is more natural: it is natural—tribal, aboriginal—to embrace all members of society in equitable fairness. The success and stability of social democracies—which describes all leading nations—is proof that, for all its flaws, the progressive approach produces the "greatest good for the greatest number."

Conservatism is psychologically unnatural. It rests on fear: not only the ubiquitous existential insecurity, but additional personal fears. These fears may be impressed by the higher self into the psychic template; or may arise from childhood experience. One such fear is of attack, or an insidious, creeping harm; coupled with a feeling of childlike weakness and vulnerability: paranoia, in a word. Often a deep conviction of personal evil permeates the psyche. The fear of authority figures and their power is strong.

Again, personal psychology is first, political philosophy second. A conservative psyche, projected onto the world, sees what? A world swarming with evil; *evil* being one of the conservative's favorite words. Because they feel innately evil, by projection they view the entire human race, if not all of Nature, as evil. Their feelings of vulnerability manifest in typical ways: they see a world swarming with threats and enemies: communists and terrorists targeting the Homeland; illegal immigrants overrunning the border; Islam menacing Western Civilization; criminals running amok in the streets; and their response is *retreat*: retreat behind walls of wealth and weaponry; throw a solid wall across the border; fill the bunkers with nuclear weapons; sleep with a loaded gun by the bedside. Feeling personally powerless, they take refuge in emblems of power: guns, tanks, and barbed wire.

Taking our analysis deeper, what is the source of all the flux and dynamism in the world? *Why* should the world be forever shifting and changing? Why can't Nature just hold still? At the very root of Nature lies *impulse*. In deepest terms, impulse originates from the primal pulsation—on-off, on-off—of the camouflage system. Though it whirs beneath your senses, this primal pulsation sets up the dynamic of life. With every "off" pulse, the material realm blinks into nonexistence; when it blinks back "on," the subatomic elements forming the system have shifted ever so slightly, which in turn creates a new "picture" of the world. In simple terms, then, *impulse is life*; stasis is death.

The conservative fears impulse. Often this fear arises in child-hood, where the inquisitive child's curiosity and innocent impulses bring rebuke, even pain, teaching the child to fear and self-censure its impulses. Innocent exploration of sexual organs, explosions of song and dance, vigorous racing about—all the natural activity of the happy, curious child—are squelched, banned, suppressed: for they disturb the staid adult world. Another source of impulse repression is school, where children are forced to endure an unnatural stasis in their seats. Another source is religion, especially a religion preaching the doctrine of Original Sin—*you were born evil!* the child is told, a festering sump of malevolent impulse.

Whatever the source, the outcome is a psyche fearing impulse. Impulse means change, dynamism, flux; so conservatives seek a rigid stasis in society, throwing the brakes on progressive expansion and clinging to Today—or, better yet, Yesterday. A psychological rigidity suffuses the conservative mind and psyche.

Deeper still, the conservative fears Nature. What is Nature but free-flowing impulse? No grand overseer orchestrates the harmony and dynamism of Nature; no one orders the plants and animals and seasons about. As bizarre as it may sound, Nature's very freedom and exuberant impulse threaten the conservative. There is no one in charge, no one giving orders, no one policing and jailing—no one controlling the system, reins in hand—it just works, perpetually dynamic and spontaneous yet stable.

No one consciously says, "Nature's free-flowing impulse threatens me," but it is so: for what else explains the conservative's desire to control, dominate, tame, pave, and destroy Nature? This is often justified under the guise of "progress," of extracting "natural resources" for human benefit; but often no economic benefit drives what, to nonconservatives, seems a willful, perverse delight in blighting and wounding Nature.

Conservatives love death. If impulse is life, and they fear impulse, then they fear life itself and embrace its negation, death. Again, this is rarely conscious. But conservatives are always clamoring for war—they form the perpetual War Party in every time and place; they support the death penalty; they love guns, cops, and military machinery; their engagement with Nature often involves killing wild animals.

Because progressivism is psychologically natural, we need spend less time exploring its roots and expressions. A child grows into a progressive naturally—that is, unless adults inculcate a fear of impulse, the instinctively communitarian ethos of the tribe shines undimmed. Compassion for the less fortunate, and a conviction that government's role is to ameliorate their suffering, is the natural outlook, the progressive outlook, which is generally shared by the people of modern nations.

Where the psyche is tainted with feelings of lack or deprivation—often of love or fairness—the natural progressive outlook may harden to a needy recasting of the parent-child relationship, this time with the wounded "child" running the show. Progressive activists, particularly of the militant stripe, are often projecting a personal psychodrama onto the world, and by "saving" others, win temporary relief from their early wounds. They replay the wounding drama, with themselves in the adult savior role, orchestrating the outcome and winning ephemeral relief.

Both progressives and conservatives are guilty of selective aphasia. They believe they perceive the world clearly, and think and act rationally; but because fear is irrational, wherever fear lies, reason flees. Conservatives ever clamor for more cops, more tanks, more fighter planes, more soldiers, more bombs, more border guards—more emblems of security to assuage their howling vulnerability. Outsiders can only stand apart and scratch their heads with wonder: we already have enough firepower to destroy the planet many times over—*how much more do we need?* Further, because of their belief in human evil, conservatives champion moral crusades—temperance, the war on drugs, abstinence sex education, ad infinitum—as reins on evil human impulse. *What exactly are they afraid of?* reasonable people can only wonder—*why the hysteria over private behavior?*

Progressives, especially those driven by "savior" psychodramas, can similarly bewilder those not so driven. The endless call for more social programs catering to the less fortunate, and the demand for more funding for existing social programs—with never a thought given to accountability—vexes those outside the progressive circle. *Are people not responsible for anything?* others wonder. *Must the government carry us in a gilded chariot from conception to death? Must every potential danger to body and mind be scoured from the Earth? Are we that helpless, that fragile, that indolent?*

Both camps are fiscally irresponsible where their private fears lie. The conservative hunger for civil and military weaponry is never quenched—it cannot be, since it arises from irrational fear. The progressive quest for an all-inclusive social safety net is similarly never fulfilled. Both camps would spend their treasuries into bankruptcy before applying reason and judgment to their fear-goaded goals. In some countries, the treasury is far beyond bankruptcy into massive deficit—and still the spending continues unabated.

Political Dynamism and Equilibrium

In tribal societies, authority is held by elders who mature naturally into their leadership. In civilized societies, however, that natural authority is shattered, for a society of millions cannot be so governed. Instead, a hierarchy of power develops, and certain questions must be answered: who holds the power? how do leaders gain and lose power? how is it transferred? how vertical is the power relationship? how much relative power do leaders and the populace hold? and so on.

As mentioned, authoritarianism is the "natural" political order. A supreme leader at the top, surrounded by a small cadre of trusted aides, runs the country by edict. A vast police force maintains civil discipline. A strong military repels enemies and marches out on conquest. Such a system assuages existential insecurity because it is rigid, stable, and consistent. Everyone knows what to expect; everyone knows the penalties for misbehavior. Civil liberties, artistic license, freedom of travel and movement—all are subjugated to the all-important Order. Authoritarianism is the "natural" political order of civilized society—the natural response to endemic insecurity—and most nations and empires, historically and in present day, have been governed by it.

Democracy is a recent creation—with a few ancient exceptions—and is a much more fluid, dynamic system because it (theoretically) invests power in the populace; "leaders" are to implement the will of the people. Robust civil liberties, artistic freedom, unhindered movement, a free press, leaders selected by popular vote after open debate, the military under civilian rule—these are the features of democracy. Democracy is unnatural because it inverts the power pyramid: the people dictate, the leaders follow.

Because democracy is unnatural, much more dynamic and unstable than authoritarianism, it requires the people's strong commitment to its endurance and a willingness to let the political system, rather than groups or individuals, determine its course. For equilibrium to be maintained amid the cacophony of progressive and conservative voices, all sides must be willing to present their views in the marketplace of ideas, there to be embraced or rejected. No one takes up arms to force the society around to his views—that is domestic terrorism.

Equilibrium is maintained in democracy by oscillating between conservative and progressive positions. Over years and decades, democracies tend to swing from one pole to the other. Because no political philosophy can realize utopia, the great middle-of-the-road mass tires of one or the other political extreme and votes for its contrary. A great push-pull dynamic underlies democratic societies—

progressives pushing society forward, conservatives pulling it back—and over time, society inches slowly forward.

Again: authoritarianism is natural, democracy is unnatural. Left to their own devices—given absolute power—both progressives and conservatives will fashion authoritarian states. The conservative utopia is well-known—the military dictatorship, the fascist Fatherland—while the twentieth century belonged to progressive "workers' paradises"—the Soviet Union, North Korea, Cuba: all failed states. Only democracies enjoying a vigorous debate between progressive and conservative camps—and arcing between them to find the middle ground—can endure, prosper, and offer maximum liberty and opportunity to its citizens.

Progressives are naturally comfortable in democracy. Open-minded, tolerant, inquisitive, they thrive in the roiling atmosphere of political debate, artistic innovation, and fresh ideas. Conservatives, to the contrary, are uncomfortable in democracy. The free flow of people and ideas, the bewildering and offensive artwork, the justice system skewed toward individual rights—these offend those convinced of human evil. Evil must be controlled with strong measures, force, and law: not coddled, not left free to spew offensive ideas, not allowed to violate social standards with impunity.

As mentioned elsewhere, the Earth rides its own arc of accelerating and decelerating vibration. Yours is an age of accelerating vibration—else you would not be literate and able to read these words—meaning root human consciousness is accelerating as well, gradually growing more expansive and inflected with spirit. In such a time, the progressive philosophy is better aligned with the Earth's acceleration: the happiest society is one that mirrors that acceleration with its own, that gradually embraces a higher and more expansive vision.

Both progressive and conservative perspectives are essential for society to maintain stable equilibrium, even as that equilibrium shifts forward or backward as power arcs from one camp to the other. When progressives leap forward, conservatives slam on the brakes. When conservatives retreat, progressives check their regression. This is the dynamic of democracy. Over time, however, the progressive side wins: it always wins, as long as a society is aligned with Earth's acceleration.

Looking back over recent centuries, consider the striking changes in the world: slavery has been abolished; women granted suffrage; children barred from working and provided free education; civil rights granted to marginalized groups; environmental protections enacted. Each step of this gradual evolution has been championed by progressives and resisted by conservatives. Again, the two are permanent psychological types, even as the issues of the day evolve from era to era. Progressives seek *embrace*: embrace of the downtrodden, minorities, women, children, gays, Nature; welcoming everyone into the circle of affiliation, seeing they are respected and cared for. Conservatives seek *retreat*: they resist widening the circle, resist the liberal granting of rights, resist inclusion and acceptance.

It is tempting to say, then, that progressives are always right and conservatives are always wrong. In the long run, this is true. The happiest society is one aligned with Earth's accelerating vibration, embracing the flowering potentials of human consciousness. Certainly the heroes of history were all progressives: the Founding Fathers were radical revolutionaries; Lincoln freed the slaves; Muir founded the conservation movement; Roosevelt launched the New Deal; Parks, Kennedy, and King fulfilled Lincoln's promise by enhancing civil rights.* If conservatives are remembered at all, it is with disdain for their obtuse backwardness, their assaults on civil liberties and Nature, their resistance to expanding the circle of affiliation, their blindness to social trends. Conservatives play an essential but thankless role in democracy, always championing the wrong side of history.

Democracy is a phase in human evolution. Because it is unnatural, ultimately it must be superseded—either by regression to authoritarianism or by evolution into a higher form of social organization. That higher form will resemble tribalism, being the natural human social order: meaning the decline of massive nation-states and a return to smaller-scale society. What that evolution will look like— a smooth transition or calamity—lies in your hands, and in your descendents'.

---

* We speak through an American; but every country has a similar lineage of progressive heroes.

15

The Enlightened Warrior:
Healer of the New Age

As we close this book, we wish to encourage you on your path as "enlightened warriors" bringing about a more evolved and harmonious world. We first describe the qualities of the enlightened warrior, and then offer suggestions for preparing yourself in body, heart, mind, and spirit, so you may offer a healing, stabilizing energy to the rocky process of cultural transformation.

The Enlightened Warrior

Let us tease apart the seemingly oxymoronic phrase "enlightened warrior." Traditionally, warriors are aggressive, testosterone-fueled fighters wreaking havoc on their foes. We offer a new definition: one who resists the forces of division, destruction, and alienation which now permeate your world, and who brings healing energies to one's sphere of influence. Thus, the enlightened warrior's approach is both passive and active, physical and spiritual. It is the passive refusal to participate in and support ongoing ecological and cultural disintegration; and the active embrace of healing, harmonious, spiritual life principles.

It is symptomatic of the old order that it views strength solely in material terms, in the size of its armies and number of its warheads. The dawning new order views strength quite differently: as the degree of receptivity an idea finds among those hearing it. For it is understood that consciousness creates manifested reality, and where a concept finds a large and welcoming audience, that idea edges closer toward physical expression. This, then, is the "secret weapon" of the enlightened warrior: recognizing that refusing to participate in ongoing cultural battles is not a sign of weakness, but of strength; for by denying such battles your energy—whether for or against—you bleed them of intensity, thus lessening their endurance and impact.

When your leaders launch yet another needless war to boost their popularity and enlarge their global empire, it may seem that people of consciousness should take to the streets in protest; to counter war energy with peace energy. Yet this is itself an "old order" approach; for it unconsciously assumes the old-order focus on size and numbers: how many people took to the streets, how many letters and calls were made, poll numbers, etc. What the advocates of peace don't realize is that they *strengthen* the old order by protesting its militarism, for resistance is energy, and the target of that energy is vitalized for the resistance.

The true enlightened warrior's approach to military madness is passive, not active: refusing to fight, refusing to participate in "patriotic" displays of flag-waving and chest-thumping; and refusing to participate in peace rallies, where venom is directed toward leaders. If everyone simply refused to fight—not protested angrily, just simply refused—there could be no war.

This is not enough, however, for the coming times promise seismic upheaval as the old order stubbornly (and increasingly desperately) strives to retain its grip on power, wealth, and prestige, even as its foundation crumbles beneath it. As calamitous events erupt with greater frequency, the instinctive reaction is to collapse in fear, to isolate oneself from the larger turmoil, to narrow one's focus to mere survival. This mindset fortifies the old order, as the old order is rooted in fear. What is needed is a consciousness so clear and pure, so flexible, so adaptable, that it can ride the roller coaster of cultural upheaval with its clarity of vision undimmed. This is the consciousness of the enlightened warrior.

For many who study metaphysics, their experience rarely goes beyond intellectual abstraction. They revel in contemplating profound and uplifting ideas, having rejected conventional dogma, but less often do they become more genuinely spiritual in their thoughts and deeds. The blockages to translating spiritual ideas into a spiritual life are many: emotional wounds, physical ailments, the workaday grind, a culture indifferent to genuine mystical insight. The problem is that now, and more so in the times to come, merely commanding an intellectual grasp of the unfolding transition will be inadequate to cushion your increasingly rocky journey. At all levels of being there must be a purity, a clarity, a suppleness, allowing you to ride the transition with minimal disorientation.

We have written elsewhere about the vibrational "set point" acquired at birth which determines the intellectual and spiritual framework of those born at that time. The set point is a vibrational pattern encapsulating the earth and cosmic energies extant at the time of your birth; its pulse binds you to others of your generation in a common range of experience, defining the upper and lower limits of potential spiritual and intellectual growth.

Because the planet is in a phase of accelerating vibration, the older you are, the slower your set point pulses vis-à-vis younger generations. While this crucial determinant of consciousness cannot be changed, there are many things you can do to keep yourself flexible and adaptable in the times ahead.

Healing Emotional Wounds

In your current understanding, it is believed that memories from childhood are stored in the brain and that talking with a counselor about unpleasant memories brings emotional healing. It can. The model is flawed, however: memories are not stored in the brain; they are lodged within the "memory field," one of the various energetic layers encircling the body. If there are "wounds" from childhood (or any time), they are not simply neuronal artifacts sparked to life by a therapist's probing; they have a physical reality as matrices of discordant energy carried in the memory field.

This has several repercussions. First, it means that all incoming vibrational information is distorted for passing through the discordant memory field. Now, no one ever absorbs pure, unadulterated vibrational information because the higher self has sculpted many patterns into the energy fields which filter incoming energy. But these discordant memory matrices can severely scramble incoming information to the point that the mind's interpretation is radically distorted, almost to the point of having no relation to the original perception. This obviously interferes with effective manipulation in the world.

As an example, a child attacked by a dog may grow into an adult with an irrational fear of dogs. The most benign and loving canine will be regarded with a shrinking panic. Likewise, a girl who resents her abusive or indifferent father may grow up to regard all men as abusive philanderers—and seek out relationships confirming her prejudice. Dogs and men come in all varieties, but a discordant energy field can shrink that variety down to monochrome caricature.

Second, it means that energy projected outward is similarly distorted as it passes through the discordant memory field. Whenever you speak to someone, your words and gestures are but part of your transmission; for your words and movements carry the subtle energetic imprint of your essential self. You have had the experience of meeting someone and instantly liking or disliking him—to a far greater degree than seems natural on first meeting. Whenever two people meet, their energetic fields overlap and entrain. Where harmony and resonance result, you feel instant rapport; where the overlapping fields clash and grate, you can't wait to break away. A distorted memory field, festering with unhealed wounds, screams "toxic! toxic!" to those you meet.

A third effect is that carrying these distorted memory matrices can affect the body's health. Ideally, the body is surrounded by a cocoon of harmonious, integrated energy fields which support its health and healing. When those energy fields are distorted and disharmonious, they can no longer support the body: they may even damage it.

The deepest, most comprehensive healing of emotional wounds would supplement the traditional therapeutic "talk" approach with healing and dissolution of the discordant matrices lodged in the memory field. As few in your society are even aware of the existence of the memory field, at present there are scant options for such healing. Our host has had the experience of working with a healer who directed spirit guides to conduct such healing; among the families of spiritual entities coming to the service of humanity at this time are those who specialize in just such emotional healing. Working through a healer, they diagnose the nature of the wound and then meticulously reweave and repair the energy patterns so they are once again harmonious with the larger fields. The work is very subtle and intricate and the client rarely feels anything specific occurring during such a healing session.

Unfortunately, one cannot heal oneself in this regard because even if one could draw down a pure energetic "template" of the wounded region, that template would be distorted just for passing through the extant wounds. It is necessary for an individual who does not carry similar wounding to facilitate the entities' work. It would be possible for two friends of reasonably developed intuitive faculties to heal each other in this regard, though a full description of the process lies beyond this essay.

Healing the Body

We have mentioned the body's vibrational set point fixed at birth. While this energetic foundation cannot be changed, one can keep the body supple, flexible, and dynamic, the better to harmonize with the planet's accelerating vibrations. Because there can be only so much of a gap between the body's energetic condition and the upper reach of consciousness, it is important not to neglect the body on the path to becoming an enlightened warrior.

Obviously, the single greatest determinant of the body's condition is the food you put into it. If we may propose a modification of the classic food groups, it would be as follows: "earth foods," "water foods," and "air foods." Bedrock (earth), water, and air are the three essential elements of the earth system, and they are the constituents of every food source. Their relative proportion determines whether a food falls into the earth, water, or air category. It is most healthful to eat from the food groups in relative proportion to their presence in the body; this means about 20% earth foods, 70% water foods, and 10% air foods. Earth foods are dense and relatively dry: root vegetables like carrots and potatoes; legumes and grains. Water foods are most fruits and vegetables grown above ground, as well as animal flesh and eggs. Air foods are light and ethereal: some flowers and blooms; dried seeds (like dandelions), even manmade concoctions like popcorn and cotton candy.

We do not wish to join the interminable debate over what constitutes a healthful diet (you see, we are deliberately withdrawing our energy from the controversy!). The ideal diet for you is a product of your gender, constitution, age (set point), activity level, and locale. Beyond trying to eat in the proportions outlined above, try to eat only as much as you need to maintain ideal weight. An overweight condition interferes with the energy fields encircling the body.

If the body is to remain receptive to accelerating earth vibrations, it needs to be flexible. Flexibility can be maintained either through stretching exercises or gentler activities such as yoga. It is important that all muscles be regularly stretched lest they harbor energy blockages.

Have sex regularly, with yourself if a partner is not available. This does not apply if you are an old soul who genuinely has no need for such activity, and you will know it. For everyone else, it is a fallacy that celibacy is somehow more "spiritual" than a vigorous sex life. In fact, sex is one of the most important aspects of keeping your body and energy fields toned, flushed, and harmonized. Sex with a partner brings a vigorous energetic exchange, an openness and receptivity to outside energies, that aids in absorbing fluctuating earth energies. It also invigorates and stimulates the body overall. It is one of the most important elements of moving the body toward "enlightened warrior" status.

Healing the Mind

The modern mind is often a tangled clutter of plans, dreams, conflicts, decisions to be made, decisions regretted, and the pressure of having too many things to do and not enough time to do them. In addition, the media beam endless images of carnage and suffering from around the world, and lavishly detail the failings and peccadilloes of politicians, all of which contribute to a sense of powerlessness and cynicism. If such a mind could be graphically depicted, it would appear as a ball of static with occasional pockets of lucidity tucked within its frazzled folds.

Because you are mental creatures and your world is the outward manifestation of your inner life, it is crucial that the aspiring enlightened warrior turn down the static and boost mental clarity. New ideas will come trickling into awareness, individually and collectively, and to receive the proper consideration they must have space to grow and be heard. A mind staggering under the pressures of daily life will be ill-equipped to consider the relative merits of new ideas.

One step in the process is to try to dampen down emotional reactions to events, especially distant events in which you have no direct interest. When you grow angry at reports of war or devastation across the globe, you clutter your mind with the intense energy of anger, and contribute that anger to the global pool of consciousness. One alternative is to project sympathy rather than anger at those whose actions disturb you. When reading accounts of genocide or burning rainforests or murdered children, instead of growing angry, try sympathy instead: "You poor souls, you have no idea what you're doing." Sympathy comes from a higher place—a godly, compassionate place—than anger, so you reduce both the emotional charge in your mind and the anger energy flowing into the global pool.

An even better option is to reduce or eliminate awareness of disturbing events outside your sphere of influence. What need have you to know of the suffering and travails of those around the globe; isn't your own life, your family and friends and community, compelling enough? Limiting your awareness to events in your immediate area, which any registered voter holds at least some power to affect, reduces mental clutter and the sense of impotence the global media have fostered.

As far as daily life goes, it is wise to cultivate a detached, almost whimsical attitude to the pressures and conflicts which arise. One might even take the "deathbed perspective": "When I'm lying on my deathbed, will what's happening now really matter?" In a few cases the answer is yes; in most it is no. Taking the deathbed perspective helps to bleed some of the intensity from life's routine ups and downs, thereby reducing the frazzle in the mind. It is a serene peacefulness we seek to cultivate as enlightened warriors, the better to keep ourselves flexible and adaptable, and to contribute our soothing energy to the global pool.

Healing the Spirit

In the deepest sense, of course, the spirit does not need healing; it is pure and beyond degradation. What needs healing is one's relationship with spirit, the channel between spirit and waking consciousness. If the enlightened warrior is truly to be enlightened, that channel must be free of blockages and static. Here lies perhaps the greatest challenge facing the aspiring enlightened warrior.

The challenge arises largely because of the setup of earthly existence: your waking consciousness is designed to ensure your physical survival first and foremost, and to do so it focuses almost exclusively outward, onto the physical realm. This naturally "squeezes out" more subtle streams of guidance flowing from spirit. It is almost paradoxical, therefore, to speak of becoming "more spiritual" in everyday life because the setup of waking consciousness militates against allowing spiritual flows to permeate the mind.

There are, however, ways to enhance the flow from spirit to waking mind. One is to follow the steps outlined above for healing the mind: reducing sharp emotional responses, reducing awareness of distant events, taking the deathbed perspective. Another is to deliberately open the channel between spirit and mind. There are several ways to do this.

One is to make a regular practice of opening oneself up to spirit. The most common technique is meditation. Here the waking mind, while fully conscious, becomes an empty vessel that spirit can fill. Meditation is not entered with any specific intent that a given issue be addressed, but simply "paves the way" for greater communication between mind and spirit. It also dampens the chattering of that incorrigible chatterbox, the ego.

Another technique is to utilize the spirit-mind channel to receive specific information. Rather than simply opening oneself up, as in meditation, here the channel is activated for a specific purpose. One appropriate use would be to ask for guidance from the higher self in making simple decisions, decisions which can be reduced to yes or no. Taking a few moments to quiet yourself and rest comfortably, ask aloud for guidance in making a decision. Assign "yes" to your right index finger, "no" to your left index finger. Try not to "anticipate" which answer will be received, and try not to influence the process by hoping for one or the other; simply state the decision to be made and assign neural pathways for spirit to indicate its response. You will be surprised at how a finger will seem to pop up with no deliberate intent on your part.

Should you always follow the advice you receive? Of course not: you must still retain your waking deliberative faculties. Spirit does not have feelings to be hurt by your choosing another path. The point is simply one of creating a bridge of respect between mind and spirit; that you would take a few moments out of your day to seek spirit's guidance in making decisions helps to fortify that bridge.

To recultivate that deep connection with the spirit realm, take some time to be in Nature. Like a pagan of old, assign a god-personality to every element of creation: to the wind, the rain, the sun, the night, the plants, the animals. Feel the natural world swarming with sacred consciousness; a theater of the gods. This is not a cute exercise; it is your essential reality. The enlightened warrior knows he or she never walks alone, but is enveloped in a warm cocoon of spirit, a world swarming with life! life! sacred life!

Healing your relationship with spirit depends on first healing the other aspects of being—mind, body, and emotional wounds. Only when the mind and body are fully harmonized and humming at peak vitality can the connection with spirit be similarly vitalized. In the meantime, of course, spending time in wild Nature automatically helps to heal and harmonize the body and still the mind, essential elements of the process.

Riding the Roller Coaster

What is the purpose of following the scheme we have outlined to harmonize body, heart, mind, and spirit? The purpose is to ensure a flexible, adaptable, supple total being which can ride the roller coaster of cultural transformation without surrendering to fear or panic. As the transformational process continues, it will become more challenging to maintain a sense of personal security and serenity. As you know, we shy away from making concrete predictions, but the broad outlines of the process are clear enough. Let us look at a few manifestations of the larger system in which you are involved.

Ecology. The natural world is a harmoniously interwoven system of self-regenerating cycles which maintain balance and stability. This ensures a sturdy, predictable "platform" for plant and animal life. Because every ecological system has built-in redundancies and backup systems, it is not immediately apparent when Nature is damaged by human activity; the depth of the damage can be masked by the compensatory backup systems. At some point, however, even the backup systems become overtaxed to the point where they can no longer compensate for further damage. At this point the ecological system begins to unravel, no longer regenerates itself, and cannot support its population of living forms.

This "breakdown" point—where the previously masked damage is laid bare in severe consequences—is being reached to varying degrees around the globe. As little pockets of ecological health are destroyed, the larger fabric unravels, and disturbing global patterns emerge. At present the most obvious and worrying of these is global warming (which we discuss elsewhere), but there are other less obvious, but equally serious, patterns of decline. The number and severity of storms—hurricanes, tornados, cyclones, typhoons—grow as the system cannot disperse its energy in less disruptive ways. Drought, rising sea levels, temperature extremes, and desertification all interfere with food and water production. Ultimately, food and water supplies decline and the human population cannot sustain its burgeoning numbers.

One can easily project the consequences: civil and international wars over food and water, widespread starvation, a stark gap between well-fed "haves" and starving "have nots," a retreat from international cooperation into every-country-for-itself selfishness, lowered intelligence among undernourished children: in short, a globe of misery.

Society. Any system built on a foundation contrary to natural law must ultimately collapse. Since the entire edifice of western culture—and, indeed, any civilization—is based on a core value of separation, which violates natural law, the many political, economic, and cultural expressions of that value must fail. This process of cultural decline, which ineluctably plays itself out regardless of the Earth's underlying energy, quickens in a time of accelerating energy. The loss of faith in traditional religious institutions, and the scorn and cynicism engendered by politics—religion and the state being the twin pillars of civilization—bespeak a decline in social cohesion.

A society is sustained only when its members derive benefits from the system commensurate with the energy and taxes they put into it. When the system is seen as indifferent or even hostile to the aspirations of its people, the system must crumble. No one staged a revolution to force the dissolution of the Soviet Union; it simply disintegrated because its "workers paradise" was a nightmare of repression detested by its citizens. That level of hatred is not yet seen among democratic countries, where the power to vote carries some small sense of ownership, but the increasing alienation many feel toward large cultural institutions means energy is being drawn away from them, portending their collapse.

In a time of social upheaval, when security seems to be swept away, the natural reaction is fear. Fear engenders fascism, the iron grip of the state forcing society to function with cold efficiency and stability, enforced by the firing squad. Fascism need not arrive in jackboots and tanks; it can creep upon a society slowly, crushing its liberties one by one in exchange for a promised security. If such seems impossible in your democracy, study the "war on drugs" and "war on terrorism" and how willingly your society has surrendered its liberties in exchange for the "security" of a drug- and terrorist-free society (and has the government delivered its half of the bargain in exchange for your constitutional liberties?).

Another clue that disintegration of the old order is accelerating is the hysteria, violence, and rising madness among those clinging to the old order, the conservative wing. Those who surrender to fear—the antithesis of reason—and desperately try to force society to revert to an imagined state of blissful cohesion act not from reason but from fear. Because fear is such a powerful emotion, it can grip its listeners in a frenzy of panic with its seductive warnings of societal collapse, terrorist triumph, swarming migrants, and divine damnation. It is axiomatic that everything conservatives do accelerates, rather than reverses, the process of cultural disintegration, because actions motivated by fear inevitably bring about the opposite of the desired outcome.

Relationships. Interpersonal relationships are the sine qua non for the vast majority of humanity. Through the trials and challenges of relationships—family, friendship, romance—you learn, you grow, you suffer and exult. Family and friends provide the crucible in which you play out the grand themes of human life.

In eras of quiescent vibration, relationships are easily maintained; the bumps and grinds intrinsic to any relationship are smoothed out by the underlying foundation of solidity. In an age such as yours, when energy accelerates dynamically, it is much more difficult to harmonize two souls in a lasting union. It is as if relationships were cast into a centrifuge, and only the most ideally matched souls can withstand the forces tearing at them.

In such an era, it is likely that many will experience a gnawing dissatisfaction with life; a prickly discomfort and malaise. The real source of this dissatisfaction is the jarring discrepancy between the accelerating energies of the planet and the individual's energy patterns, as rooted in the set point, but no one experiences it this way. Instead, they search for the source of their unhappiness in their job, their friends, and their families. Desperate to ameliorate their itching discomfort, they may jettison whole aspects of their lives—abandoning long-time spouses, their children, their work—in a quest for healing. And they may find that doing so results in some temporary or long-term relief, for in breaking long-standing patterns they may align themselves in closer harmony with the Earth's shifting energies, forge a deeper connection to spirit, and align themselves more closely to their life purpose.

The point is that relationships are often the casualty of a search for healing and balance, though the abandoned individuals are not the true source of discontent. This accounts for the high divorce rate, the reluctance of many to commit to marriage, the casual indifference to children. It is important to recognize that this need not be the case, that long-term relationships can still flourish amid the centrifugal pressures; in fact, many find their relationships to be their sole refuge in a world swirling with disorder and alienation.

Into the Future

Where does this rather grim scenario leave the enlightened warrior? Right where he or she can always be found: in a place of serenity, contentment, awareness, compassion, and love. The enlightened warrior understands the larger process of which he or she is a part and is not disturbed by the chaotic upheavals of cultural transformation. The enlightened warrior relishes the chance to participate in an era as exciting and dynamic as that bridging old and new social orders. The enlightened warrior serves as a magnet to those seeking calm and stability in their lives; a haven of serenity amidst the chaos.

The enlightened warrior makes a special effort to cultivate relationships with young people. Knowing that the younger generation has many "starbabies" carrying accelerated energies aligned with the future, the enlightened warrior offers guidance and hope, lest they be overwhelmed by rising cultural chaos and surrender to cynicism. For such young persons—and the enlightened warriors who guide them—are the seeds from which will sprout a new order founded on harmony with natural and spiritual principles.

Our blessings on your journey.